THIRSTING AFTER GOD

THIRSTING AFTER GOD

Keith A. Price

CHRISTIAN PUBLICATIONS
CAMP HILL, PENNSYLVANIA

Christian Publications, Inc.
3825 Hartzdale Drive, Camp Hill, PA 17011
www.cpi-horizon.com
www.christianpublications.com

Faithful, biblical publishing since 1883

Thirsting after God
ISBN: 0-87509-820-7
LOC Control Number: 99-080104

00 01 02 03 04   6 5 4 3 2

Cover photo by Larry McKee

DEDICATION

To

Rosemary,

my life's partner
and dearest friend,
who has modeled for me
by her Christlike life
the truths
I have so inadequately
put into words.

*It was said of Samuel Rutherford that he had
"A thirst no earthly stream could satisfy;
A hunger that must feed on Christ or die."*

CONTENTS

PART ONE   "THIRSTING"

"The mirage shall become a pool" (Isaiah)

PART TWO   "CRAVING"

"My soul thirsts. . . . My body longs" (David)

PART THREE   "PLEADING"

"Now show me Your glory!" (Moses)

PART FOUR   "CONTEMPLATING"

"Beholding . . . we are transformed" (Paul)

PART FIVE "YIELDING"

"Present your bodies!" (Paul)

PART SIX "SEARCHING"

"Search as for hidden treasure" (wise father)

Rabbit Trails for Digging Deeper

Foreword

W hile I've never met A.W. Tozer, I can tell you I know Keith Price.

Just out of university, I arrived in Montreal to head up a youth ministry. What a challenge! I was beyond my depth and I knew it. But happily I met Keith Price. In what became a door-opener to evangelism in Quebec, "Sermons from Science" at Expo '67 was a remarkable success—in large part because of Keith's vision and heart.

In that early sojourn, I learned much from Keith, not only about leadership, but what voracious study for knowing and making known the Word of God can do.

Some years later our lives intersected again as we worked together in a national Canadian ministry. It was then that I learned more of what is at the heart of good Bible preaching and teaching. To watch Keith stand before people, Bible open (and no notes!), exploding with enthusiasm for what God has to teach us, is a picture etched in my memory. Often now as I stand to open the Word of God, that picture frames my thoughts and I pray, *Lord, by Your Spirit bring this, Your Word, alive today.*

Recently, at the college where I serve, we invited Keith to give a week of lectures to first-year students. Age differential was not an issue. The barriers of age, culture, lingo and image were crossed with ease. Enthusiasm for the Word was birthed in the life of those students; it came naturally from the life of my thirsty friend.

Thirsting after God is a great title—one which so well matches what I've learned from this great expositor of the Scriptures. He has lived this theme, modeling it to so many of us across North America and around the world.

In the dryness of your life today, allow these seminal thoughts to direct you away from the mirages of life to the only true Source, Jesus Christ our Lord.

—Dr. Brian C. Stiller
President, Tyndale College & Seminary
Toronto, Canada

AUTHOR'S PREFACE

For six years after Dr. Tozer's death, I pondered just what he had meant when he frequently talked to me about thirsting after God. The term I understood, but the depth of longing he spoke of was something beyond me.

I had been preaching for seventeen years before I understood experientially in 1969 that my thirst for the written Word, valuable though it was, needed to be surpassed by my thirst after God Himself. But when it finally hit me, it gripped me for life!

This book, drawn from messages I have preached on this theme since that time (over thirty years ago), shows the journey I have taken and the lessons I have learned along the way. However, I have approached each of the Bible passages covered in this book with the dynamic of the written word rather than that of the spoken word, attempting to keep the flow casual and largely conversational. In essence, each of these chapters conveys many of the more important concepts I have enjoyed preaching in various ways over the years.

I have on more than one occasion been stunned to read in a previously unread Tozer book some concept which I had thought was my own. The thoughts he drilled into me in my formative years are scarcely, if at all, separated in my mind from what I was gleaning personally from Scripture.

In the light of this, I feel quite sure that many a thought, concept or turn of a phrase appearing in these pages will have originated either with Dr. Tozer or others whose wisdom I have devoured over the years. It is virtually impossible for me to sort these out, as would doubtless be the case with most writers of similar experience. I know my readers will understand and, where necessary, let me know, so a particular oversight will not be repeated.

It is not just because it is conventional courtesy that I wish to express my deep thanks to those who have sacrificed time and energy to ensure the manuscript was finished as planned. My wife, Rosemary, not only patiently bore my silence of preoccupation as I grappled with the text; she also quietly got on with tackling my share of domestic and garden chores (which even in normal times is, because of so much travel, considerably less than her own share). In addition, her love since childhood of reading, syntax, grammar and spelling was just what I needed in those many extra hours she spent patiently checking.

I do want to thank my three children, Melinda, Mark and Julia, together with their families, for reading, suggesting ideas or concepts I had forgotten or omitted and also for technical help (computers, etc.) in the various stages of the book.

It took my long-time colleague Brian Stiller three attempts over the years to persuade me to get down to business putting into writing some of the messages he had heard me give. I am deeply grateful for his encouragement and also for his willingness in a busy life to write the foreword.

Even then, I may not have started had it not been for the gracious offer of two dear friends that they arrange for our needs to be met while I took months away from my regular work of preaching and teaching. In this matter, I am particularly indebted to Tom, Karen, Miller, Bob, Fred and Jack.

It was indeed a great encouragement to know that the publishers of almost all the books by my mentor, Dr. A.W. Tozer, would want to publish mine. It brings me even closer to him. It has been a joy to work with Christian Publications. My editors, George McPeek and Janet Dixon, who also thirst after God, have been most understanding, not to mention objective and helpful at all stages of the book.

Lastly, and most important of all, I want to thank the Lord Jesus Christ, who by His Spirit has given me every strand of understanding I have of this grand theme. I know I have only scratched the surface of this exciting search into the heart of God. But because some might feel they understand even less than I, I am encouraged by the fact that 'in the land of the blind, the one-eyed man is king'!"

To God be the glory!
Keith A. Price
Victoria, British Columbia, Canada

Introduction

MY MORNINGS WITH TOZER

The streets of Toronto became hallowed ground on those special mornings. Though he was widely read, he taught me to become a man of one Book. He showed me how to march out of step, to contradict my generation. I learned how to stir that holy fire within my heart and in the hearts of others. He inspired me, by frequent quotations, to read the great hymns of Bernard de Clairvaux and to pray them as I thirsted after God.

Yes, Tozer was my model, my example. He spent time with me. He was patient with me. He prayed for me. He taught me to redig the old wells; to call people back to the old paths and to maintain a healthy suspicion of fads and novelties. He profoundly influenced my life and ministry and I shall be eternally grateful.

"Had a letter from New York this morning, inviting me to a spiritual summit conference," said the legendary A.W. Tozer as he stepped into my car. Unsurprised by this strange conversation-opener from the man who wasted little time on verbal niceties, I said, "How interesting!"

Tozer looked at me disapprovingly. *"Interesting, young man?"* Then, obviously concerned lest I consider such a letter something to be valued, he discharged a one-liner put-down I shall never forget. "If you think you're at the top," he said, "it's a sure sign you're at the bottom!"

I got the message. And not wanting to get trampled further, I simply said, "Yes, Dr. Tozer!"

It was just one of hundreds of unforgettable biblical principles I was to learn from this man who knew God like nobody I had ever met.

That was 1961. I was thirty-one and already privileged to have spent the occasional morning with Tozer in my car as I drove through Toronto streets on business. Robert's Rules of Order were just not his cup of tea, and I may have been his convenient excuse to get out of staff meetings at Avenue Road Church (later Bayview Glen), where he was the preaching pastor after thirty-one years in Chicago. But it grew into a habit and we enjoyed many such mornings together during those last two years of his life.

It started when I went to see him for counsel on how to balance my time between the pharmaceutical business, family responsibility and preaching several times a week. Whereas I cannot recall his answering me on the purpose of my visit (he rarely did!) he quickly noticed I was thirsty for God. I was soon to realize that in the providence of God, I was with the man who, probably more than any other on the continent, could show me how to cultivate that thirst.

I used to pick him up at the church at 10:30 and drop him off at his home in Old Orchard Grove around 2. As we talked between business calls—and more lengthily over lunch—he would pour himself into me, teaching me the greatest lessons I have been privileged to learn.

Little did I realize the profound effect these times would have on my life and preaching in the years ahead.

Some who knew Tozer remember him for his candid, sometimes abrasive manner. I remember him for his pursuing single-mindedly "the surpassing greatness of knowing Christ Jesus," his Lord.

Though an evangelical mystic with a consuming passion for contemplative communion with the living Christ, he had little time for mincing words. Yet, despite his chosen lack of so-called diplomacy (by which he understood "hypocrisy"), this man of great theological insight thirsted after God more than anyone I have ever known.

Tozer taught me to be suspicious of the crowd mentality. I can hear him still: "Young man, when you see a horde of Christians running toward a bandwagon, turn on your heels and run as fast as you can in the opposite direction!" That opposite direction was, as he foresaw forty years ago, swimming against the stream of hyperactivity to a place of solitude and communion with God.

He poured that longing into me and showed me I could pursue it no matter how formally uneducated I may be. One day I asked his advice on further education. Having left school at fourteen, I felt neither adequate nor comfortable when invited to teach in academic institutions. Should I go back to finish high school—and more? "Young man," he said, "you have a hunger for God. You are busily engaged teaching the Word. In my observation, many like you who go back to finish their education never regain the ministry momentum they had. Keep on pursuing God on your own."

Then he added unforgettably, "I too left school at fourteen. We would both have enjoyed a campus experience. Yet we have one thing going for us that many people lack."

"What's that, Dr. Tozer?" I asked.

With a twinkle in his eye he retorted, "We *know* we don't know, so we keep on trying to find out!"

To spend time with Tozer was to be exposed predominantly to his contagious thirst for God Himself. From his tutoring (as a mystic rather than a schoolman) I now find myself able to call almost any message "thirsting after God," no matter what page of the Bible I preach from.

Tozer started by showing me that my thirst would make me long to contemplate the majesty of God. He lamented the loss of the concept of majesty in the human race. Respected monarchs, he felt, were valuable stepping stones to understanding God's majesty. But when respect for them is lost, the notion of majesty is warped and the understanding of God is shrouded in confusion. This quickly results in the worship of worship, something Tozer saw as a self-serving substitute for the worship of the King of kings.

He dismantled that mechanistic caricature of conversion, which stakes everything on the initial decision. He knew that a crisis not followed by a process becomes an abscess. He foresaw the danger of how-to manuals that announce peace to those who follow instructions (whether they feel it or not). They give only a false sense of security built on a formula rather than a real work of God. Such victims, he said, would have but little longing for God.

And even where there was real evidence of conversion, Tozer was careful to warn of the dangers of thinking one had arrived. He would agree with Abraham Heschel that "he who is satisfied has never truly craved" for God. Drinking from God's ocean, he said, would serve only to deepen my thirst. So I would have to go back again and again.

Tozer filled my mind with the classical writings of St. Anselm, Nicholas of Cusa and Julian of Norwich. He taught me to ponder and use the rich hymns of Bernard de Clairvaux and Frederick Faber, kindred spirits in thirsting after God.

He also demolished my wariness of contemporary non-Protestants by frequently quoting from the wisdom and contemplative insights of G.K. Chesterton or Thomas Merton (with whom he corresponded), although by no means agreeing with all they wrote.

One of his favorites was Gerhard Tersteegen, that saintly mystic who, 200 years before Tozer, had modeled for him the commitment that says, "My soul finds rest in God alone."

Dr. Tozer linked me with the past. He gave me an addictive taste for the writings of some of the Church fathers. He taught me to thirst after God. I shall be forever grateful.

PART ONE

Thirsting

"The mirage shall become a pool"
(Isaiah)

Remain in me, and I will remain in you.
No branch can bear fruit by itself; it must remain in the vine.
Neither can you bear fruit unless you remain in me.

I am the vine; you are the branches.
If a man remains in me and I in him, he will bear much fruit;
apart from me you can do nothing.
(John 15:4-5)

PRAYER FROM A THIRSTY BRANCH

The year was 1977. I was alone. It was late in the evening. I was sitting up in a hospital bed, having been prepared for major surgery the next morning. Knowing that I would be under a general anaesthetic, the rare possibility that I may not come out of it did cross my mind.

I became increasingly conscious of my complete dependence upon the Lord. I recall that evening thinking back over my life. *If this were my last day, could I say that I had lived a life of conscious dependence upon God?* I was grieved as I thought of many times when I had gone my own way, or tried to do God's work in my own strength.

I confessed and repented. I again asked God for the privilege of a new start. I vowed that if He brought me through the surgery, I would become more diligent in pursuing the means of grace and thus drawing upon His strength.

I reviewed some long-ago-learned verses from my old King James Bible, since then replaced with a modern version. They brought back vivid memories as I could recall the exact spot I was when I had learned many of them. And so it was that in that centuries-old mind-set and language of the King James Version, I found myself penning a prayer which expressed my dependence on and longing for God.

It may also express your longings too, as we come to our first thoughts about thirsting.

O Thou, who art the Vine,
    from whom this feeble branch of mine
    receives its life,

So draw my dried and empty roots
    deep into Thine all-resourceful heart,
    that, so o'erflowing with Thy grace,
    my heart may crave and find
    none other Source, save Thee.

So teach me with contentedness to lean
    on Thy sufficiency,
    that I may learn
    it is not work, but rest,
    most surely shall bring forth fruit;
    that struggling is in vain,
    that Thou alone canst give,
    I, but receive.

So cause me to most trustingly abide in Thee,
    that men may see
    that what is formed from union with Thyself
    must of Thy nature take;
    and so my branch, a channel only be;
    an arm, on which Thy fruit is formed,
    a reproduction, Lord, of Thee.

So pour into my being Thy sacred sap,
    that, conscious of Thine all-pervading love
    and helpless to absorb
    the fulness of infinitude,
    my heart will cry,
    "It is enough! Lord, stay Thine hand,"

And then, and then alone,
    work Thou, most faithful Lord,

on this—
my small capacity to know Thee;
that with each hunger, and each thirst,
and with each promised filling with Thyself,
I may receive a vessel larger than before,
that satisfaction, hunger coexist,
as one ambitious thimble
      in an ocean dipped;
that I'll still thrust my branch's shoots
into Thy Vine
and so produce Thy fruit,
now larger, now more beauteous
      than before;
that I'll fulfill the purpose in Thy mind,
and, in fulfilling, find
Thy will be done.
Amen.

Isaiah 35

¹*The desert and the parched land will be glad;*
  the wilderness will rejoice and blossom.
Like a crocus, ²it will burst into bloom;
  it will rejoice greatly and shout for joy.
The glory of Lebanon will be given to it,
  the splendor of Carmel and Sharon;
They will see the glory of the LORD,
  the splendor of our God.

³*Strengthen the feeble hands;*
  steady the knees that give way;
⁴*say to those with fearful hearts,*
  "Be strong, do not fear;
your God will come,
  he will come with vengeance;
with divine retribution
  he will come and save you."

⁵*Then will the eyes of the blind be opened*
  and the ears of the deaf unstopped.
⁶*Then will the lame leap like a deer,*
  and the mute tongue shout for joy.
Water will gush forth in the wilderness
  and streams in the desert.
⁷*The burning sand will become a pool,*
  the thirsting ground bubbling springs.
In the haunts where jackals once lay,
  grass and reeds and papyrus will grow.

^{8}*And a highway will be there;*
  it will be called the Way of Holiness.
The unclean will not journey on it;
  it will be for those who walk in that Way;
  wicked fools will not go about on it.
^{9}*No lion will be there,*
  nor will any ferocious beast get up on it;
  they will not be found there.
But only the redeemed will walk there,
  ^{10}*and the ransomed of the LORD will return.*
They will enter Zion with singing;
  everlasting joy will crown their heads.
Gladness and joy will overtake them,
  and sorrow and sighing will flee away.

CHASING A MIRAGE

1

"The mirage shall become a pool."
(Isaiah 35:7, NASB with text note)

O Lord, I am so tired
    of searching for satisfaction.
You know how many times I have sought it!
The trouble is I give up too soon
    without giving it a chance!

I want this search to be different,
    and ask for the grace of perseverance.
Give me that stickability,
    until I am surprisingly convinced
    that the "it" for which I search
    is really You Yourself!

The story is told of a platoon of soldiers making their way through the Egyptian desert in World War II. The sun was merciless, the sand scorching and the water bottles bone dry.

Despite weariness and parched throats, they trudged on, assured by their guide of a nearby oasis. But the minutes turned into hours, until discouragement and desperation engulfed them.

Suddenly there was a shriek of delight. "Look!" said a young soldier, pointing in a quite unexpected direction. "There's water!"

They could scarcely believe their eyes, but sure enough, several miles away was a desert lake! With newfound energy, they made straight for the glistening water, despite the pleadings of their guide. After all, "seeing is believing."

Nearing the body of water, they found it smaller than first assessed. What did it matter? But the nearer they got, the smaller it seemed, until on arrival they found nothing but glowing sand.

They had chased a mirage—appearance without reality! Only a journal recorded their dying hours.

Many of us live disappointed lives. We were told about the "rivers of living water," but all we have experienced is a mirage, or at most a dripping tap!

Some have accepted the mirage as the norm of the Christian life. They act as though the reality does not exist, as if it is only a mirage! Not wanting to lose face, they stick with the crowd of similarly disappointed church-goers. A few secretly hope that one day they will be "surprised by joy." In any case, they go on keeping up appearances.

Others, more openly disillusioned, pursue another mirage, then another, and yet another! Ever seeking, they never seem to find the satisfaction they crave.

In Isaiah 35 the prophet has uplifting words for still-thirsty people like this. "You've been chasing a mirage? Well, take heart," he seems to say. "The reality does exist. The rivers do flow. The parched soul will be satisfied. And 'the mirage shall become a pool' " (see 35:7).

The promise does not mean that what is a mirage today will satisfy tomorrow. A false hope will never satisfy. It means rather that once we pursue God (the Pool) instead of our own lesser goal (the mirage), it won't be long before we find Him. For "there is a river whose streams make glad the city of God" (Psalm 46:4).

Thinking It Through

Think back over your life and try to recall the things, people or pursuits which you thought held out great hope for fulfillment but which you now realize were only different types of mirage.

Planting It Deep

"You will seek me and find me when you seek me with all your heart." (Jeremiah 29:13)

Praying It In

O God!
I lack the wisdom
to know what will bring
fulfillment in life.
I have pursued so many things
in vain.
Give me Your wisdom
so I will have no more wasted years.
Amen.

What Mirage Am I Chasing?

2

"The mirage shall become a pool."
(Isaiah 35:7, NASB with text note)

We are so concerned about happiness and fulfillment in life that we may waste years before realizing we have been barking up the wrong tree. Let's think about some mirages we chase.

The Mirage of Pleasure

Directly pursuing pleasure or happiness never works. Entertainment? Fun? Drugs? Alcohol? The next morning will find the booty short-lived. Such pursuits don't drown our troubles; they just teach them to swim!

Lasting happiness is a by-product, not a goal. The goal is right living. "Blessed are those who hunger and thirst for righteousness, for they will be filled" (Matthew 5:6).

The Mirage of Power

The hunger for power is widespread. But however high the rung on the ladder, we keep wanting to climb higher.

Some seek power by throwing off restraint. But true power comes not from boundless freedom, but from submission. It is one of God's paradoxes. We are free only by being yoked to Christ, the real Source of true power.

The Mirage of Possessions

Yet again, the more we have, the more we want! And the more we get, the more we leave behind. Neither getting nor leaving can bring joy.

The Mirage of Knowledge

We may be fooled for a while that winning arguments or impressing others with what we know is the route to happiness. But this often only alienates our friends! True wisdom comes only from God in His Word. He promises true happiness only to those who pursue that way of life.

The Mirage of Change

When satisfaction and fulfillment elude us, we put the blame on other people or other circumstances. "If only I could change this set-up I could find happiness!" we say. We change jobs, houses, hobbies and spouses. The fault, we feel, lies outside ourselves—someone or something else is to blame. But the usual reason is *ourselves*! And we take the problem with us wherever we go.

The Mirage of Pursuing My Inner Self

It is now popular to pursue peace by "finding my real inner self." Such psychoanalytical techniques may help us understand ourselves better, but they can do little to change us into what we long to be.

Our greatest need is forgiveness—impossible unless we choose God's way. Books urge us to ignore "outdated concepts" like guilt. We are told to reclassify sin as sickness, more readily treatable by specialists. But the festering lesion remains putrid, covered up by the prescribed band-aid. I go through the motions in vain.

The inspired psalmist asks,

> Where can I go from your Spirit?
>> Where can I flee from your presence?
> If I go up to the heavens you are there;
>> if I make my bed in the depths, you are
>>> there. . . .
> If I say, "Surely the darkness will hide me
>> and the light become night around me,"
> even the darkness will not be dark to you;
>> the night will shine like the day,
>> for darkness is as light to you.
>> (Psalm 139:7-8, 11-12).

We cannot escape dealing with God.

The problem is inside, not outside! But the real obstacle to joy is not merely within me—it *is* me! I *myself* am the problem. The capital "I" with which I am grappling is the central letter of that ugly word "sIn." The Bible is the only map to true peace. It leads to the city called Forgiveness.

Thinking It Through

Have I been chasing a mirage, truly thinking it would bring fulfillment? Or could it be that I am deliberately trying to avoid facing God?

Planting It Deep

"Why spend money on what is not bread,
*   and your labor on what does not satisfy?*
Listen, listen to me, and eat what is good,
*   and your soul will delight in the richest of fare.*
Give ear and come to me;
*   hear me, that your soul may live."*
*   (Isaiah 55:2-3)*

Praying It In

O Lord,
why couldn't I
have learned from history?
It seems I just had to
make all those mistakes myself.
One after another I have chased
useless and unfulfilling pursuits.
Now they are behind me
and I've learned my lesson.
I long to know
what will really satisfy my soul.
Please show me, Lord!
Amen.

IS MY LIFE ALSO A MIRAGE?

3

~❧❦☙~

"The mirage shall become a pool."
(Isaiah 35:7, NASB with text note)

If I am pursuing a mirage rather then life-giving water, I will bear no fruit. I will also become a mirage—appearance without reality! My life will disappoint others, not refresh them. I will have a veneer of Christianity but little or no substance.

The beautiful language of Isaiah 35 deeply impressed Handel. Lovers of his *Messiah* will recognize the words. The chapter's ultimate fulfillment is God's establishing of His kingdom partially in our hearts now, and ultimately universally.

Wherever God reigns, in the world or in my heart, He is King, and His kingdom comes. He transforms everything. The change described in Isaiah 35 will inevitably come about. Whatever comes under His Kingship—things or people—will be characterized by the five marks of His presence. They are a worthwhile test of my reality:

1. My life will become a place of beauty (35:1-2). "The desert and the parched land will be glad. . . . It will burst into bloom. . . . The glory of Lebanon will be given it, the splendor of Carmel and Sharon; they will see the glory of the LORD, the splendor of our God."

16

My life may be flowerless profession, but my desert can blossom and burst into bloom.

2. My life will become a place of strength (35:3-4). "Strengthen the feeble hands, steady the knees that give way; say to those with fearful hearts, 'Be strong, do not fear. . . .' "

God will empower me with courage to endure under trial. He will fortify me to resist temptation. He will give me His strength to serve Him by placing His powerful hand in the otherwise limp glove of my life.

3. My life will become a place of miracle (35:5-6). "Then will the eyes of the blind be opened and the ears of the deaf unstopped. Then will the lame leap like a deer and the mute tongue shout for joy."

God is the Healer of the outside and the inside. He gives sight to the spiritually blind and makes the inwardly deaf hear His voice of guidance and direction. Those who listen will walk in His ways, worship in His house and witness to His resurrection. For He loves to cause mute tongues to shout in worship and witness.

4. My life will become a place of holiness (35:8-9). "And a highway will be there; it will be called the Way of Holiness. . . . Only the redeemed will walk there."

He lifts me out of life's gutter and starts me out on his highway of holiness, "the paths of righteousness." Those who have not yet submitted to God's cleansing from sin cannot find that road. Only the redeemed can travel on it and be protected. It is the Christian life.

5. My life will become a place of rejoicing (35:10). "The ransomed of the LORD will return, they will enter Zion with singing. . . . Gladness and joy will overtake them, and sorrow and sighing will flee away."

God's Spirit will infuse me with the very life of Christ thus giving me His fruit of joy. The monotonous and the humdrum will be revolutionized. I will burst into song—"the song of the soul set free." "Sorrow and sighing will flee away."

Verse 7 especially encapsulates the miracle God will do for His land and His people. It describes the landscape in four phrases: wilderness, desert, burning sand and thirsty ground. Isaiah, guided by the Holy Spirit, says that in such a place—yes, even your life and mine—there would gush forth water, streams, springs and a pool.

It is nearly half a century since Dr. Martyn Lloyd-Jones first drew my attention to Isaiah 35. He explained that "the burning sand" is more correctly rendered "mirage." So in the midst of disappointment and inevitable death, the promise rings out loud and clear: "the mirage shall become a pool!"

Thinking It Through

Is it possible that my life itself is also a mirage? Am I in fact a counterfeit—appearance without reality? Am I pretending to be someone I really am not?

Planting It Deep

"Therefore, if anyone is in Christ, he is a new creation; the old has gone, the new has come!" (2 Corinthians 5:17)

Praying It Through

O Lord,
I have been living
for so long
in the lowlands of mediocrity.
I am disappointed and fed up.
I simply can't keep up the show
any longer.
I want my life to count;
I want to be like Jesus.
Would you show me then
just what I must do?
And also give me the strength
to do it?
Amen.

FINDING THE SPRING OF LIVING WATER

4

*"My people have committed two sins: they have forsaken me,
the spring of living water, and have dug their own cisterns,
broken cisterns that cannot hold water." (Jeremiah 2:13)*

Six hundred years before Jesus came to earth, God spelled
out man's perennial problem through Jeremiah: "My
people have committed two sins: they have forsaken me, the
Spring of living water, and have dug their own cisterns, broken cisterns that cannot hold water" (Jeremiah 2:13).

A broken cistern brings the same disappointment as a mirage. Both look like they can satisfy. But while the one springs
a leak and holds no water, the other never was anything but
"appearance without reality."

Life's most important bridge is the one that leads from mis-
directed searching into faith in Jesus Christ. And it may take a
time of true heart-searching before we are willing to cross that
bridge. When we are ready, we will find God was right all the
time. The older we get, the harder it is to admit it, for we are
really saying, "I wasted all those years stubbornly following
my own inclinations." But a wise man will admit mistakes and
make changes for the future right up to his death.

We will not be ready to take such a leap until God the Holy
Spirit gives our consciences no rest. Maybe we will not be able

to stand a haunting conscience any longer. It will then take two steps to bring it about. Both are enlarged on in Jeremiah 2:13.

Stop going to the broken cisterns.

Broken cisterns are our own chosen paths. When we stop going, our change of mind is what the Bible calls "repentance"; it is a turning away from previous goals by an act of the will. This is not mere remorse, which involves only the emotions. Nor is it just regret, which is better, but still limited to the mind and the emotions. But when God "commands all people everywhere to repent" (Acts 17:30), He expects such to affect the mind, the emotions and the will.

Turn to the Spring of Living Water.

We do this by giving Jesus Christ the right to run our lives. After all, He is the One who paid our debt on the cross. Without such payment we could never be forgiven or have our guilt removed. We must be willing to tell Him we have blown it and want to start over with a new life.

Then we say thank you with our lives, not just our words. This turning to Christ the Bible calls "faith." For the past, God graciously grants us forgiveness; for the future, He gives us the Life of His Son. And it is He, the living Christ, who is the Spring which satisfies. We open our mouths wide and let Him satisfy our thirst by regularly listening to God in His Word and talking to Him in prayer, just as if He were visibly in the room with us.

What is to stop you doing that right now as you are reading this book? The words from here on will then have real meaning for you. You can invite Jesus to run your life right where you are. There is no need to go to a church and kneel down in a pew—although that could be valuable if you need help. Why not use a well known hymn-prayer and open up to the God who already knows what is happening in your mind and heart? Just say to Him:

> I tried the broken cisterns, Lord,
> But ah! the waters failed;
> E'en as I stooped to drink they fled
> And mocked me as I wailed
>
> Now none but Christ can satisfy,
> None other name for me;
> There's love and life and lasting joy,
> Lord Jesus, found in Thee.[1]

Thinking It Through

Life has so many "broken cisterns" that hold no water. Most of us have tried enough of them. The Lord Jesus promises He is the Spring of Living Water. He alone can satisfy the longing soul. Are you yet willing to give Him a chance?

Planting It Deep

"But if serving the LORD seems undesirable to you, then choose for yourselves this day whom you will serve, whether the gods your forefathers served beyond the River, or the gods of the Amorites, in whose land

*you are living. But as for me and my household, we will
serve the LORD." (Joshua 24:15)*

Praying It In

Lord Jesus,
I here and now
invite You into my life,
as my Savior from sin.
I accept the forgiveness You offer
because You paid my debt.
I also acccpt You
as Lord and Master of my life;
the One I will serve.
I accept from Your hand
whatever You choose
to allow across my path—
because I'm committed.
Amen.

EVEN CHRISTIANS CHASE MIRAGES!

5

"The mirage shall become a pool."
(Isaiah 35:7, NASB with text note)

Those who have come to faith in Christ will have learned how to bypass a mirage. But even Christians can chase a mirage of a different kind. I suggest four:

The Mirage of Decisionism

Several years ago my wife and I drove with some friends to Yellowstone National Park. I had heard much of this world-class park with its breathtaking scenery and natural phenomena, especially Old Faithful.

Arriving at the park entrance, we pulled up to the ticket booth, only to be told the park restaurants had closed for the season. The attendant suggested we go back to the town and have lunch. So, no sooner had we entered the park than we swung around the tollbooth and went out again.

Seeing the obvious illustration of the Christian life, and with tongue in cheek, I said to my friends, "What a disappointment! They build it up so much in the advertising but when you get inside it's nothing but a tollbooth! I'll have to tell my friends, 'I've been to Yellowstone and it just doesn't measure up!' "

An alarming proportion of those who make a "decision" for Christ get no further than the gate. What a caricature of conversion. A disappointment! A mirage! A "decision to follow Christ" means following Christ! We must not stand still, gloatingly waving an insurance policy to heaven. We are to keep on going ever deeper into "the park" (as we did later!).

The Mirage of Traditions

I often meet those good-living people who devote themselves to the peripheral things of church practice. Nobody told them Christianity is Christ. Yet others, from Bible-believing churches, get caught in the trap of good, Christian habits—meetings, seminars, committees and programs. These good things can become ends in themselves, substitutes for God. The enemy of the best is the good. But the good is not good enough to sustain a vibrant Christian life.

The Mirage of Experience-Hunting

How easily we can get "hooked" by some passing fad: a new how-to book, a dynamic speaker, a miracle worker or newly publicized phenomena in a church across town. Genuine Christians often flit from place to place expecting God to break through the clouds and zap them with some new celestial two-by-four!

Each venture, initially promising, bursts like a bubble in their hands. A.B. Simpson surely saw the trap when he wrote, "Once it was the blessing, now it is the Lord." He had stopped chasing the mirage!

The Mirage of "Having Arrived"

In other mirages, we substitute something for Christ. Here, however, we are pursuing Him so eagerly we become consumed with vanity—the vanity of the "right choice," that of ardently pursuing God. Feeling we have outrun others, a condescending sense of superiority takes over. We think we've arrived! But this arrogance indicates we are anywhere but deep into the heart of God.

If, however, we avoid that trap, Satan's next ploy is to make us believe that because we did, we must be deeply spiritual. We think mistakenly that the ungodly thing that grips us is God's Holy Spirit. But God's Spirit brings humility, not pride.

Once we believe that our most recent experience is the ultimate, we will no longer hunger and thirst. Thinking we have "arrived," we ourselves will then become just another mirage. We shall begin to stagnate in our fellowship with God.

Thinking It Through

The pursuits of the mind, the will or the emotions can—any one of them—make me think I am on the right track. But the life of God in the soul will properly motivate all three.

Planting It Deep

"Not that I have already obtained all this, or have already been made perfect, but I press on to take hold of that for which Christ Jesus took hold of me. Brothers, I do not consider myself yet to have taken hold of it. But one thing I do: Forgetting what is behind and straining toward what is ahead, I press on toward the goal to win the prize for which God has called me heavenward in Christ Jesus." (Philippians 3:12-14)

Praying It In

O Lord,
as I look back on my life,
I see I started well,
but have not kept on growing
in the things of the kingdom.
Would you continually prod me
by your Spirit?
I determine today
that by Your grace
I will keep on moving
closer and closer
to Your heart.
Amen!

I Too Chased a Mirage!

6

❦

"The mirage shall become a pool."
(Isaiah 35:7, NASB with text note)

Prior to becoming a Christian in 1950, I was involved in top-secret work in Southeast Asia. I also pursued journalistic sports writing and refereeing with a passion. Obsessed with these things, I would eagerly grasp every opportunity to climb the ambition ladder. But each rung brought repeated frustration. There were always more rungs beyond.

On becoming a Christian through a letter from my believing mother, I threw my weight into Christian work. I even started to teach my referee students. But while it was Christian work, it failed to satisfy my longings.

One day I realized I needed to be more involved with God's people. The fellowship and example of other Christians was surely very near to the heart of God. *After all,* I thought, *people are more important than programs!* Somehow, I expected the people themselves would meet my need for fulfillment. When two of them badly let me down, I became discouraged.

One weekend it was my turn to oversee the security of the classified establishment where I worked. Locked inside, with no assignments, I poured myself into reading John 13-17. I shall never forget those two days! God opened up His Word to me in an amazing way. He gave me more understanding than I had got in nearly two years as a Christian.

From this point, my Christian ministry moved ahead with more focus. Moving back to Bristol, England, I was soon preaching in churches of several denominations. My passion for the Word grew enormously. I would often study it for four hours a day. God's work and God's people were important. But God's Word was supreme.

We moved to Canada in 1959. In my introduction to this book I wrote of the mornings I spent with Dr. A.W. Tozer between 1961 and 1963. He warned me of the danger of "a sterile textualism," and urged me to go "beyond the sacred page" to God Himself. The written Word, he said, was meant to lead me to the Living Word. It was not be an end in itself.

That conversation sparked six years of wondering if I were still chasing a mirage. The importance of the Bible was indisputable and Tozer would have been the last one to disagree. But it was the realization that meditation on the written Word should grow into contemplation of the Living Word which kept driving me to Christ Himself.

One night in 1969 I had an unforgettable experience in Minneapolis, related in segments 13 and 14 of this book.

My relationship with Jesus Christ took on new meaning. A newfound love and a new vitality characterized my ministry. I realized that what I had pursued for nineteen years as ends in themselves were meant to be but aids to bring me nearer to Him. It soon dawned on me I had anything but "arrived."

It was this realization which then kept me diligently using the means of grace which God had provided for me to cling to Him. Not as ends, but as means!

Thinking It Through

Could it be that I am at a standstill in my faith? Am I only an activist who loves to be involved in Christian work, or a gregarious person who loves to have fellowship with Christian people? Is that my limit of involvement? Maybe I consider myself superior because I delve daily into the Word. Is the written Word driving me to Jesus, the Living Word? What is my next step?

Planting It Deep

"Find rest, O my soul, in God alone; my hope comes from him. He alone is my rock and my salvation, he is my fortress, I will not be shaken." (Psalm 62:5-6)

Praying It In

O Lord,
I have come to realize
that being active in Your work,
being socially inclined
or being studious by nature
does not make me a disciple.
I confess that
I have tried to find satisfaction
in Your work, Your people
and even in Your Word alone.

I thought my love for them
was love for You.
I now see that the Hub of Your wheel
is Your Son, Jesus!
And so,
while enjoying these other means,
I now long for Him alone
to be the Center of my life.
Amen.

PART TWO

Craving

"My soul thirsts . . . my body longs"
(David)

He who is satisfied has never truly craved,
and he who craves for the light of God neglects his ease for ardor,
his life for love,
knowing that contentment is the shadow,
not the light . . .

And when the waves of that yearning
swell in our souls,
all the barriers are pushed aside.[1]

A Prayer

Lord, as I expose my mind
   to Your great truths,
   will You open the eyes of my heart?

Show me the timelessness
of these inspired words.
Help me to see myself in them.
Give me an increasing longing
to know You.

Help me to focus
on what I can understand
rather than worrying about what I can't,
knowing that when I come back
to read it again,
it will become clearer.
Amen.

Psalm 63

A psalm of David. When he was in the Desert of Judah.

¹O God, you are my God,
   earnestly I seek you;
my soul thirsts for you,
   my body longs for you,
in a dry and weary land
   where there is no water.

²I have seen you in the sanctuary
   and beheld your power and your glory.
³Because your love is better than life,
   my lips will glorify you.
⁴I will praise you as long as I live,
   and in your name I will lift up my hands.
⁵My soul will be satisfied as with the richest of foods;
   with singing lips my mouth will praise you.
⁶On my bed I remember you;
   I think of you through the watches of the night.
⁷Because you are my help,
   I sing in the shadow of your wings.
⁸My soul clings to you;
   your right hand upholds me.

⁹They who seek my life will be destroyed;
   they will go down to the depths of the earth.
¹⁰They will be given over to the sword
   and become food for jackals.
¹¹But the king will rejoice in God;
   all who swear by God's name will praise him,
   while the mouths of liars will be silenced.

THIRSTY AND DESPERATE

7

"My soul thirsts for you, my body longs for you, in a dry and weary land where there is no water." (Psalm 63:1)

"There's a God-shaped vacuum in all of our hearts." So said Blaise Pascal 300 years ago when he realized only God could meet his longing. No more mirage-chasing for the perceptive French philosopher. He thirsted, drank and thirsted for more!

As David, king of Israel, writes Psalm 63, it has been many years since he took his first drink from the Fount of Living Water as a boy. He has had a lifelong relationship with God. Yet his ongoing thirst can hardly be contained. He keeps on pursuing God. He longs to know him better. He never seems to get enough of Him. His vacuum too was God-shaped!

You also may already have come to faith in God, yet, despite the transaction, your thirst persists. In fact, the more you drink from the Fountain the more thirsty you become. Don't worry! The enigma of your ongoing thirst is a sign of life, not death.

Your initial thirst was a thirsting *for* God; but your present, constant, still-not-satisfied longing is best described as "thirsting *after* God." It is a thirst by a finite being for the infinite God. The healthier you are spiritually, the more thirsty you will become. Abraham Heschel was surely right when he said, "He who is satisfied has never truly craved."

And yet there is a certain satisfaction in the actual thirsting itself. The longing, in its own right, becomes a source of joy and delight. To be fully satisfied would in one sense rob me of that delight. Perhaps this is one reason why God ensures the longing just does not go away. The beautiful verse that says, "whoever drinks the water I give him will never thirst," is, we shall see, not contradictory, but complementary.

I know of no passage of Scripture that echoes my own yearning for God like this psalm. It expresses the inner longings of my heart. It also gives me insight into why my thirst is so intense and why I become more thirsty, rather than satisfied, when I drink from the Fountain.

At one time in my life I began each morning by reading this psalm. It was the morning psalm of the post-apostolic church, the psalm with which the singing of psalms (the sacred songs or hymns) was introduced each morning as worship became more formalized.

David is at one of life's low points. (They come to us all!) He has been forced militarily from both his palace and God's house and is likely fleeing in exile from his son Absalom, who was trying to snatch the throne. (You can read about it in Second Samuel 15-19.) He arrives at a desert hideout and longs more than anything for a renewed sense of God's presence.

My trouble may be about relationships, finances, health or other areas of my personal life. David's was military. But while our circumstances may differ, God does not change every time the problem changes. He is always the same. Because this is God's Word, I can confidently apply the same principles David did 3,000 years ago. Are you willing to try?

Although it expresses longing and delight, it ends with a growing confidence in God in a time of trouble. We don't thirst just to have an ecstatic thrill tingling in our bodies. It is so we can find confidence in God to move ahead in faith.

I normally love to see a psalm in its entirety; at very least one verse. But if I tried to pack it all in here, we would miss so much of the teaching of this wonderful verse. Because it is filled with help on how to cultivate my thirst for God, I am going to break a good habit. We shall take our time on this great journey of discovery. Launch out with me then—into the deep!

Thinking It Through

While still paddling in the shallows of this psalm, I need to reaffirm my determination to put each of its wonderful thoughts into practice. Am I willing to wade out until I can bathe myself in each new revelation God is waiting to give me? If so, I shall need to learn how to swim in the deep of God's ocean. That takes time—and practice. Am I willing to try?

Planting It Deep

"The precepts of the LORD are right,
*   giving joy to the heart.*
The commands of the LORD are radiant,
*   giving light to the eyes. . . .*
They are more precious than gold,

than much pure gold;
they are sweeter than honey,
 than honey from the comb.
By them is your servant warned;
 in keeping them there is great reward."
 (Psalm 19:8, 10-11)

Praying It In

O Lord,
It has taken me so long,
but I am at last realizing
that only You
are the answer to my thirst.
I now have a sense of excitement,
an anticipation of discovery,
as I launch out into the deep.
You have promised
to reward my search.
And confidently, I leave myself
in Your hands.
Amen.

O GOD!

8

"O God, You are my God." (Psalm 63:1)

As we focus in on the opening words, it would be good to read this inspired psalm once more. As you read, walk in the psalmist's shoes. Imagine what it feels like to be in a tight squeeze. Maybe it would help to think of trouble you yourself have gone through, or may be in right now. If it were your psalm, would you say this to God?

Maybe I am conscious of something that has come between me and God. If I am to benefit from the psalm, this needs to be confessed and forsaken. We always need such cleansing before we can expect God to illuminate our minds and empower us to live. In this way, problems can lead to a deeper communion, rather than hindering it.

Some 200-year-old words from the inspired pen of Gerhard Tersteegen come to mind. They have been a great help to me in searching my own heart:

> Thou hidden love of God, whose height,
>> Whose depth unfathomed, no man knows,
> I see from far Thy beauteous light,
>> And inly sigh for Thy repose;
> My heart is pained, nor can it be
>> At rest till it finds rest in Thee.

What is there more that hinders me
  From ent'ring to Thy promised rest;
Abiding there substantially,
  And being permanently blest?
O Love, my inmost soul expose,
  And every hindrance now disclose!

Is there a thing beneath the sun,
  That strives with Thee my heart to share?
Ah, tear it thence, and reign alone,
  The Lord of every motion there!
Then shall my heart from earth be free,
  When it hath found repose in Thee.

Tell me, O God! if aught there be
  Of self, that wills not Thy control;
Reveal whate'er impurity
  May still be lurking in my soul!
To reach Thy rest and share Thy throne,
  Mine eye must look to Thee alone.[1]

Now read on, making each expression in the psalm your own. Just as the hymn expresses your heart's longings, similarly the Psalms, the hymnbook of the early Christians, can become your own prayers to the Lord. If your longing for God made you pick up this book, the superb language of our psalm's first verse will likely echo your own desire.

O God!

I find it helpful to say these two words and stop. Close your eyes! Kneel if possible. Think about what you are doing in addressing God. Repeat the words several times. Pause in between. But remember that Christianity has no place for Hindu-style mantras, magical incantations, or working ourselves up into a frenzy. The true God looks at our hearts, not our words.

You may find yourself, as I sometimes do, inadvertently thinking of the first word as if it were spelled "Oh!" I often give expression to that word when I find myself not knowing what to pray. It is simply the outward vocalizing of an inward sigh or groan. "Oh, God!" Trouble may have overwhelmed me. Such an expression brings the comfort of knowing I do not have to handle it alone. It is a reminder that God the Comforter is in it with me.

"O God." Addressing Him brings me right into His throne room. Imagine being there—a sinful person standing before a holy God. "Do not come any closer," God said (to Moses). "Take off your sandals, for the place where you are standing is holy ground" (Exodus 3:5).

What a privilege! What an awesome responsibility!

Thinking It Through

Further ponder God's awesomeness! Find a quiet spot and simply listen—in the silence, without background music or television. Close your eyes and imagine yourself before His Throne. God is in His rightful place—on that throne! You in your rightful place, at His feet! Worship Him! Don't hurry!

Planting It Deep

"I saw the Lord seated on a throne, high and exalted,
and the train of his robe filled the temple. Above him

were seraphs, each with six wings: With two they cov-
ered their faces, with two they covered their feet, and
with two they were flying. And they were calling to one
another:

'Holy, holy, holy is the LORD Almighty;
  the whole earth is full of his glory.' " (Isaiah 6:1-3)

Praying It In

O Lord,
I stand in awe of You.
I drop to my knees;
I fall prostrate
at Your feet.
Your greatness
and Your holiness
boggle my mind
and touch my spirit.
I am so grateful
that I come before
a throne of grace,
not a throne of judgment;
and that I am
no longer Your enemy,
but Your friend,
All because of Jesus!
Thank You, Lord.
Amen!

YOU ARE MY GOD

9

❦

"O God, you are my God." (Psalm 63:1)

What a powerful confession this is! Can you sincerely say this to Him? Is He truly your God? If so, you will need to think through the implications. You can do this simply by putting the emphasis on a different word each time you say it. It is one of the helps I use with many verses.

Start with *"You* are my God." People, possessions or personal pursuits may have competed in the past, but now you pronounce *God* as the unrivaled King of your life!

Then move on to "You are *my* God." Not in such a possessive sense that you deny others the same privilege, but in the sense of an intimate relationship. It affirms a personal relationship, rather like saying, "The Lord is *my* Shepherd."

And then again, "You are my *God*"—He is the One I adore, and before whom I bow in worship; the One I live for, my Life Principle, the prime factor in every decision of my life.

This perhaps best brings out the meaning of "El" (the word used for "God" in this four-word declaration). It means "strong or mighty one." Having used "Elohim" in the address ("O God"), the psalmist seems now to be calling on Him to be his strength as he faces an uncertain future.

But we need to revel in this intimacy of communion before passing on to the rest of our verse. I must allow my meditation to grow into contemplation. But how do I do it? The duties of the day call and there is much work to be done. Ponder it as long as time allows; but remember that the secret is really to find a way to keep the awe of that wonderful relationship alive throughout the day.

I have to remind myself frequently to translate the minutes of meditation into the hours of work and daily routine. If God is truly my God, He will affect everything I do throughout the day. Then far from taking *from* my employer, I will have much more to give.

Some years ago, I heard a Chinese Christian leader testify to God's goodness under persecution. Arrested because of his faith, he was taken daily from his prison cell to his assigned task—cleaning out a large cesspool in a rural area. Prisoners on other assignments would be closely watched by the Red Guard, but not this one. The foul smell was too much for them and they stayed far away.

And so it was that each morning, as he arrived at the cesspool, he would lift up his eyes and voice to heaven and start singing in Chinese:

> I come to the garden alone
>   while the dew is still on the roses,
> And the voice I hear, falling on my ear
>   the Son of God discloses.
> And He walks with me and He talks with me
>   and He tells me I am His own,
> And the joy we share as we tarry there,
>   none other has ever known.[1]

The special intimacy he had cultivated with God was so strong that he no longer noticed the vile smell. Even the cesspool had become a fragrant garden. He then proceeded to do his work as unto God. And nobody lost out!

So it is with us. The more intimate the communion, the less conscious we become of circumstances, hardships or even the passing of time. It is possible to cultivate this by means of an increasingly rich time with God each day. We can then carry the sense of His presence with us to transform the secular into the sacred.

Thinking It Through

"You are my God" is an all-committing confession which surely brings joy to the heart of God. Today, as you ponder the implications of such language, try to note the things you say and do which may cause God to question the reality of such a surrender.

Planting It Deep

"The LORD is my shepherd, I shall not be in want.
He makes me lie down in green pastures,
he leads me beside quiet waters,
he restores my soul." (Psalm 23:1-3)

Praying It In

O Lord,
while I do revel
in this intimacy
I have with You,
I don't want
to abuse it,
by forgetting
just who You are.
As Your child,
I sit on Your lap,
in sweet communion,
But as Your subject,
I fall at Your feet
in worship and adoration.
Almighty God,
King of the Universe,
Father and Friend,
I praise Your Name!
Amen.

FOUND—BUT STILL SEEKING

10

"O God, You are my God, earnestly I seek you." (Psalm 63:1)

Having expressed his devotion, the psalmist now does something about it. He earnestly seeks God! We may well ask, "If God is already his God, then why is he still seeking Him?" But that's like asking about a newborn: "She's already breathed once, why does she need to keep doing it?" Like physical birth, spiritual birth is a triggering mechanism which sets in motion a whole lifetime of worship and aspiration after God.

As I write, I can almost hear Dr. Tozer breathing down my neck: "Young man, just because you've found God, that's no reason to stop seeking Him!"

How colorfully Tozer describes some people today:

> Paul was a seeker and finder and seeker still. They seek and find and seek no more. After "accepting" Christ they tend to substitute logic for life and doctrine for experience. For them the truth becomes a veil to hide the face of God; for Paul it was a door into His very Presence. Paul's spirit was that of the loving explorer. He was a prospector among the hills of God searching for the gold of personal spiritual acquaintance.[1]

Sad to say, many people's experience of God could be encapsulated in just one crisis. But "conversion" to Christ means only that my journey to knowing God has begun. The process will take a lifetime—and then some! If God has truly wrought a work in my heart, I will inevitably be drawn to Him in increasing measure. As a baby keeps crying for its mother, so I will long for an ever-deepening communion with God.

Christians used to call that special time each day to focus our thoughts on God "the morning watch." "Earnestly" in our verse is "early" in most versions. The most quoted authority translates it "at night, when the morning dawns."

> A cithern—an ancient guitar—used to hang above David's bed; and when midnight came, the north wind blew among the strings, so that they sounded of themselves; and forthwith he arose and busied himself with the Torah until the pillar of the dawn ascended.[2]

This may well have come from three biblical statements of David: "At midnight I rise to give you thanks for your righteous laws"; "My soul waits for the Lord more than watchmen wait for the morning"; and "I will sing and make music. Awake, my soul! Awake, harp and lyre! I will awaken the dawn" (Psalm 119:62; 130:6; 57:7-8).

A rabbi comments, "The dawn awakens the other kings; but I, said David, will awake the dawn." You can almost hear the alarm going off!

Due to the typical aches and pains of an aging body, I find I have to press the "snooze" button two or even three times in the morning. But once the hot water of the shower hits the spinal cord, my grudging seems to turn to joyous anticipation of meeting the Lord in the Word during my "morning watch." If we mean business, we must cultivate a habit—morning, noon or night. This should be no "God-slot" to which He is limited. Every hour in the day and every day in the week is His and His alone.

In 1649 Nicholas Herman joined the Carmelite community in Paris as their cook. He disliked kitchen duty and longed for a life of contemplation and prayer. He reveled in chapel worship and, reluctant to return to his work, would linger as long as allowed. But gradually he learned to retain that sense of God's presence while back in the kitchen. In the end it mattered not whether he was in chapel or kitchen; he kept on thinking about God. You likely know him as Brother Lawrence, the author of *The Practice of the Presence of God*.

Thinking It Through

Think of how many "Christians" you have met who rarely mention God and who look suspicious when you express your ongoing longing for the one you both claim to know. Ask yourself: *Do I really want to become like this? Can I not take the lead and press on ahead, showing by my life that while I know God, I know also that I have still not "arrived"?*

Planting It Deep

"I will give them a heart to know me, that I am the LORD. They will be my people and I will be their God, for they will return to me with all their heart." (Jeremiah 24:7)

"Then shall we know, if we follow on to know the LORD." (Hosea 6:3, KJV)

Praying It In

O Lord,
forgive me!
For I have sometimes
treated You
as if You were a coin
I had lost,
and then found.
Having found You,
I no longer sought You.
Teach me I pray
that I have but
scratched the surface
of knowing You.
Help me to see the need
to go deeper and deeper
into Your loving heart.
Amen.

SATISFIED—BUT STILL THIRSTY

11

"My soul thirsts for you, my body longs for you,
in a dry and weary land where there is no water." (Psalm 63:1)

Having affirmed both his devotion and his diligence, David now gives us a glimpse into how desperately thirsty he is for God.

He is in "a dry and weary land where there is no water." The description puts him in the Desert of Judea, and his language is likely triggered by actual conditions there. Before the rainy season, months of drought cause the parched and cracked ground to cry out for water.

But David is thinking of his personal drought of soul. Like Psalm 143:6, he is really saying, "My soul thirsts for you like a parched land." He is desperate for God and simply must quench his thirst!

What superlative language! "My soul thirsts . . . my body longs"! In typical Hebrew poetry fashion—where the thoughts rhyme, rather than just the words—he brings these twin concepts together so we can grasp the intensity of his longing. He says, in effect: "All of my being cries out for you."

The word "longs" (in "my body longs for you") is the only occurrence of the word in Scripture. It speaks of ardent longing which consumes the last energies of a man. It means David is "pining" or "fainting with desire." It is the longing of love!

Twenty years ago I was driving a car with some friends into the Negev, the northeastern part of the Sinai desert. It was over 100 degrees. We were hot, sticky and very thirsty. What a relief when we came across an "oasis." But this was a different kind of oasis, to say the least—no water, just cola. I bought four bottles! I cannot recall the first one even touching my lips, it went down so fast. Gulp—gulp—gulp! I was so desperate I was completely preoccupied with my need.

Contrary to what we may think, this is not the kind of thirst David is speaking about. Anybody gets desperate in a crisis. It is one reason why God allows them in our lives. He knows trouble often drives us to Him and keeps us close.

No! The thirst of soul which David has is nothing less than the thirst of someone utterly addicted to God—a spiritual junkie! Someone who can hardly go one hour without satisfying that craving. This kind of thirst needs no crisis to trigger it. Those who have it are constantly and increasingly absorbed with the longing to embrace their Lover! They are driven not by crisis but by unchanging love!

Pursue with me, a moment, the thought I mentioned a few pages back. I have gradually come to appreciate that my satisfaction actually comes from being thirsty. To thirst after God, knowing I am not going to be satisfied in this life, is in itself a joy I would not do without.

I have many times wondered just how to express my enjoyment of the very desire for God in and of itself. Not until my daughter Melinda drew my attention to C.S. Lewis' *Pilgrim's Regress*[1] did I know others also experienced that same enjoyment of longing. We may well return to this thought. For in cultivating our thirst we shall find we are actually enjoying the unsatisfied thirst of becoming more thirsty.

Thinking It Through

Writing these words, I find myself asking, *How thirsty am I for this God? Does my whole being crave Him? Am I as desperate as David? If not, was I at one time? And does that unsatisfied thirst for God give me more enjoyment than physically drinking a tall glass of ice-cold water after a day in the desert?*

Planting It Deep

"How lovely is your dwelling place,
   O LORD Almighty!
My soul yearns, even faints,
   for the courts of the LORD;
my heart and my flesh cry out
   for the living God." (Psalm 84:1-2)

Praying It In

O Lord,
the satisfaction I get
from drinking from Your Fountain
serves only
to make me more thirsty.
Teach me to learn
that You are Infinite
and I, but finite.
That my vessel
can never, while on earth,
totally grasp Your greatness
or fully know Your fullness.
May this give me passionate longing
to see You, one day, as You are!
Amen.

I'VE SEEN THE MOUNTAINTOP!

12

"I have seen you in the sanctuary
and beheld your power and your glory." (Psalm 63:2)

The superb imagery of Psalm 63:1 leaves me breathless! How that man poured out his heart to God. How he longed for God. How his words echo the longing of my own heart!

What makes him thirst like that? If we are to cultivate that thirst, we need to know! Indeed he now answers the question. With extraordinary honesty, David opens the drapes on his thinking. Verses 2-5 show us the four great stimuli that drive his pursuit after God. Here, we shall consider the first one—in verse 2.

"You can see Baker today!" Just east of us, in the American Northwest, is one of our more attractive landmarks, Mount Baker, with its glacial peak glistening like a million-dollar ice cream cone. "You can see Baker" is our way of saying, "It's a great day." But sometimes guests from the East stay two or three days without seeing it because of the weather. They stare unbelievingly at us when we try to describe the view. It is hard to convince them it even exists. They've never seen it!

Ever tried sharing with others a deep experience you have had with God? Often people cannot understand why you lack enthusiasm for anything less. Once we've seen the mountain-top, we're spoiled! We can never be the same again. The mediocrity of substandard Christianity has no more appeal.

David had previously beheld God's "power and glory." It was, he says, "in the sanctuary." The word here translated "sanctuary" (or holy place) also has a greater breadth of meaning. We can be sure that David, tending the sheep in his youth, had seen God in the less formal "sanctuary" of the fields of Bethlehem. Many a time he would have sat on a rock thinking about God and composing his songs of praise (the psalms). That rock would have become to him a holy spot he would never forget.

Maybe also in this Judean desert there was a cave (perhaps the very cave he is in now!) where years before, in exile from King Saul, he had seen God's power and glory. A holy place!

Perhaps you too can recall special days when an ordinary room has become a sanctuary. I vividly remember special spots where an isolated barn or a gate overlooking a meadow or the beauty of a western beach at sunset has brought an unusual sense of God's presence. Such locations become trysting places between God and us. We expect something to happen each time we visit.

David could never forget such occasions. He says, "I have seen you in the sanctuary." (And "seen" is elsewhere translated "gazed upon"—see Psalm 27:4.) He knew what it was to "see" the Invisible and "touch" the Untouchable—for it had happened before! Yet others, who had not seen God's glory to that extent, would be far less expectant.

Last summer, on a boat near the San Juan Islands, just south of my home in Victoria, British Columbia, I thrilled to the sighting of two pods of killer whales—which our veteran skipper estimated at between eighty and eighty-five in number. As these enormous creatures gracefully surfaced and plunged, I stood against the rail, awestruck.

For a whole hour following the sighting, I gazed expectantly across the water. I knew they could reappear at any moment. Yet someone visiting the same spot later, with no knowledge of their recent presence, would have almost no sense of expectancy at all.

The theoretical possibility of a profound encounter with God rarely stimulates the adrenalin. But previous experience does. David had that! And once you've seen the mountaintop, nobody can convince you it doesn't exist.

I believe most Christians have a deep desire to commune with God in a richer way than they do. Some know it is possible. They've seen the mountaintop before! Such longing is therefore the healthy child of holy dissatisfaction. I know! I am often there!

Thinking It Through

Think back over your Christian life and try to recall those times when you felt most close to God. Did you journal them? If so, read it over. If not, why not put your memories into writing today? They may well fade fast with time. Writing them will also stimulate you to want that closeness again.

Planting It Deep

*"As the deer pants for streams of water,
so my soul pants for you, O God.*

My soul thirsts for God, for the living God.
  When can I go and meet with God?
My tears have been my food
  day and night,
while men say to me all day long,
  'Where is your God?'
These things I remember
  as I pour out my soul:
how I used to go with the multitude,
  leading the procession to the house of God,
with shouts of joy and thanksgiving
  among the festive throng." (Psalm 42:1-4)

Praying It In

O Lord,
I need to think
back over my life
far more than I do.
There is so much
to thank You for,
and so many memories
to bring me joy.
Prod me now
to recall those times
when I reveled
in Your closeness.
Then recreate in me
a longing for more.
Amen!

THE DAY I SAW THE PEAK

13

*"I have seen you in the sanctuary
and beheld your power and your glory." (Psalm 63:2)*

The year was 1967. I had been appointed commissioner of the "Sermons from Science" pavilion at Expo '67 in Montreal. During the run of that pavilion, 2.5 million people stood in line for up to five hours to see (and hear in any of seven languages) something of the wonder and majesty of God's creation. Several hundred teenagers served as volunteer hosts and hostesses. Eight thousand Canadians were trained in evangelistic counseling, many working at the pavilion.

Fifty million visitors came to Expo, and the exhaustion of sixteen-hour work days made me acutely conscious of my need to reflect Christian love.

Tozer's earthly life—and my mornings with him—had ended four years before. But his one-sentence-knock-out punches often came back to me. Irritating deadlines and growing impatience with people made me recall his warning about reducing my faith to a "sterile textualism."

The knowledge of God's Word (which grew as my preaching increased) was, on its own, simply not enough. For "if I have all knowledge but have not love, I am nothing." My lips must be backed up by my life, my creed by my character. It was this love I needed.

I questioned about a hundred pavilion workers in whom I saw this love. I wanted to know how they got it. Many were not even aware of it and were amazed I would ask. Those who knew God was in it were divided between the sudden and the gradual schools. I concluded we have a God of infinite variety who moves in mysterious ways His wonders to perform. In any case, my longing for love outstripped my caring about the means.

In 1969 I was to attend the U.S. Congress on Evangelism in Minneapolis. As the day drew nearer I had a growing longing. I left Montreal with a strong sense that God was going to meet my need.

Seven thousand leaders, mainly pastors, jammed the Congress hall. Each day increased my anticipation. The Thursday evening message touched the inner chords of my heart. The last hymn, "Spirit of God, descend upon my heart" poignantly echoed my longing for love.

Eager to get alone, I slipped out before the end, walking the ten blocks back to my hotel room. By now I was gripped with a sense of God's imminent invasion of my life. Halfway back, not wanting public embarrassment, I broke into a trot. Reaching my hotel, I hurried to Room 603. I threw my coat onto a chair and dropped to my knees by the bed.

I was overwhelmed with a sense of God's presence and convinced this was to be my night of encounter. Conditioned to avoid yielding to anything unscriptural, I opened my Bible and began reading the First Epistle of John on my knees.

Moving from anticipation to meditation in no sense diminished my awareness of God—rather, it increased it. Then, as I began to read, "Behold, what manner of love the Father hath bestowed upon us" (3:1—we used King James in those days), all heaven broke loose and God closed in on me!

Had Jesus held out His hand to shake mine (these were pre-hugging days!), I could not have been one bit more overwhelmed. Although I had been preaching for years, I had never before experienced the closeness of God like this. His loving arms seemed to envelop me, drawing me ever closer. Praise in song filled my heart and lips.

Nothing theologically controversial happened. Even if it had, I sense it would have only added to the experience. How it must grieve the Lord that we so limit Him, allowing Him to do only what we have been taught is the accepted norm. Tozer often mentioned this to me. How thankful I am that my sovereign God, without asking permission, barged through my carefully erected fences and "keep out" signs.

Almost immediately conscious of a new sense of love, but wanting to be sure its source was God, not my Welsh emotions, I decided to go to bed. If it were God, I reasoned, it would be just as real in the morning! You'll soon see that it was!

Thinking It Through

Suddenly there came on my soul something I had never known before. It was as if someone infinite and almighty, knowing everything, full of the deepest, tenderest interest in myself, made known to me that He loved me. My eye saw no one, but I knew assuredly that the One whom I knew not, and had never met, had met me for the first time, and made known to me that we were together.[1]

Planting It Deep

*"For he satisfieth the longing soul, and filleth the hun-
gry soul with goodness." (Psalm 107:9, KJV)*

Praying It In

O Lord,
"things"
can so easily overshadow
my longing for You.
I have often observed
that widows, orphans
and the dispossessed
seem to make
greater strides
in their longing for You.
I ask today for grace
to love You more than things,
that even if
they are taken from me,
I'll not give in
just because
I will then have no choice,
but because
lose them or not,
"I'd rather have Jesus
than silver or gold."
Amen.

The Morning After

14

"I have seen you in the sanctuary
and beheld your power and your glory." (Psalm 63:2)

Never before can I recall my vocal chords springing to life so quickly. I awoke at 6 a.m. actually singing, "I am the Lord's, oh joy beyond expression." I recalled the majestic experience I had before going to bed. God had broken into my life in a new way! Sensing no abating of the joy, I showered and dressed. After a precious time with the Lord, I left for the Congress Hall.

Why was each of the strangers at the elevator smiling at me? Could it be that our faces are that reflective of what's going on inside us? How I wish that attracting influence regularly characterized me.

I recall trying to analyze what I was experiencing. There was love for people, a peace which pervaded my mind and a joy that wanted to burst into song. It dawned on me that I was describing the fruit of the Spirit—love, joy, peace, long-suffering, gentleness, goodness, faithfulness, meekness and self-control (Galatians 5:22-23). Were they already beginning to take root?

We sometimes wrongly add an "s" and speak of the "fruits" of the Spirit. We settle for one fruit one day and another the next. I wonder if this could be a carnal imitation. The Bible talks of "fruit"—all together and in balance. This multiple fruit cluster is nothing less than a description of the life of Jesus. When God fills us with His Spirit He gives us this resurrection Life of Christ.

Although one part—such as joy—may predominate at a given hour, other parts, like gentleness and meekness, are ready to express themselves as opportunity demands. Is this how we distinguish the real from the spurious? Not one fruit, but all of them?

My eyes were now opened to a deeper understanding of God's infilling. I realized being filled is a command, not an option (Ephesians 5:18). It is I, not God, who normally holds things up!

I wanted to rush back to my room, to record what had happened, in case the fullness subsided or the memory faded. Now I could at least avoid the embarrassment of trying to explain what I had never experienced. But instead I walked to the auditorium and took my seat.

Imagine my surprise when the morning devotional speaker chose to speak on a comparison of the fruit of the Spirit with the Love of First Corinthians 13. It was as if God was singling me out and asking, "What does Keith need most?" I basked in the sunshine of His love.

But I was soon to go through an episode so disappointing that I would never forget it. Reveling in His love, I chose to walk alone to lunch. At the YMCA, I joined the cafeteria line-up. My new experience had not yet been tested by the strain of relationships and I was caught off-guard. Two very talkative businessmen were next to me. I am ashamed to say I found myself thinking of one of them as a "loud-mouth."

As the thought penetrated my mind and the irritation increased I became conscious of a lessening sense of God's presence. Less love, less peace and certainly less long-suffering.

Not knowing why, I slumped into disappointment. Why had God buoyed me up only to let me down? Preoccupied with my fate, I mechanically pushed my tray the whole length of the food counter, realizing when I faced the cashier that I had nothing on it. Miserable, I went around again.

As I gave (unfelt) thanks for the meal, I felt the heavy, yet wooing hand of the Holy Spirit "tap me on the shoulder." It was as if He challenged my right to talk to God. Like an illuminating flash I saw it. My thinking evil of that man had broken my fellowship with God. "The thought of foolishness is sin" (KJV). I had memorized Proverbs 24:9 as a new Christian, but never been that sensitive to this sin. To think it so grieved God that His Spirit had to fold His wings. God is holy!

Minutes later, meal untouched, I cried for forgiveness. "Lord, please teach me the seriousness of sins of the mind." He did! Gradually the joy of fullness returned.

I shall not forget the walk back. The lesson had been harsh but effective. Now I knew the infilling of the Holy Spirit was directly dependent on my confession of sin.

Thinking It Through

When I drift from closeness to God, I notice my good points. But when I am close to Him, I notice the slightest sin. Unconfessed sin prevents my being filled with the Spirit. If I do not confess, I then do not notice when I do more wrong. How can I sense his wings folding if they have not been open for some time?

Planting It Deep

"And do not grieve the Holy Spirit of God, with whom you were sealed for the day of redemption." (Ephesians 4:30)

Praying It In

O Lord,
I have learned
that if I would know
Your fullness,
I must confess my sin.
The trouble is
I am not sensitive enough
to what *is* sin.
Help me to know Your commands
that I may obey them,
And keep me
looking at Jesus' face,
so I will quickly notice
from His expression
when I have grieved Him.
Amen.

LESSONS LEARNED FROM LOOKING BACK

15

"I have seen you in the sanctuary
and beheld your power and your glory." (Psalm 63:2)

Never since that memorable night in Minneapolis have I been so conscious of God's closeness to me. Decades have passed, but I look back to 1969 as the year God blew away the clouds and let me see the mountaintop.

Meanwhile, it has often crossed my mind that if I have gone all these years without again experiencing that closeness, I must have slackened in my desire for God. I have consoled myself with the knowledge that God is sovereign and does not always respond to my penny-in-the-slot in the way expected, giving me the goodies I wanted. (Think of the years godly mothers have prayed for their wayward children.)

Does this then negate the promise which says, "When you seek me with all your heart you will find me"? No, a thousand times no! For there is something more important. Instead of giving me that satisfying sense of fullness, God still keeps increasing my thirst for him. So while there is no short-lived euphoria, like the finding of a hidden Easter egg, there is instead that profound enjoyment of a much deeper, though still unsatisfied, longing which we saw earlier.

Mark you, there is also what looks like a down-side to that. Now I am more conscious than ever of things within me which hinder the fruit of love from growing. If my love was indeed enhanced (and I feel sure it was), then dare I console myself with the possibility that my increased sense of God's holiness so heightens my recognition of sin that the gain appears more like loss?

The frightening alternative is that I have become more sinful! And writing off that possibility would merely confirm its truth!

But I now realize that the thump of His convicting heartbeat ever closer to my ear also compounds the craving to move nearer Him. I do know that when my thirst for God declines, I no longer notice the difference sin makes to my communion with Him. And that does spell sickness!

However, the point of my relating this experience is that once we see the mountaintop, we are never again satisfied with less. And doubtless, this throws light on why I keep crying out with David, "My soul thirsts for you, my body longs for you." I want to see You again, Lord, "as I have seen you in the sanctuary."

As I have thought about that special evening in Minneapolis, I realize there are a number of principles I learned about thirsting after God. Let me try and summarize them:

1. God *creates* the thirst. We must *cultivate* it.
2. When I respond, God finds a way to encourage me, often through special people or circumstances.
3. God *commands* me to be filled with His Spirit, meaning it is my move next. He will then respond to that.
4. I've noticed less resistance to the Spirit when I am alone, praying and reading His Word.

5. The fresh touch of God's Spirit can come with or without accompanying physical manifestations.

6. God has already lavished on me the love I so desperately long for. That is why I long!

7. My growing sense of anticipation is actually faith beginning to appropriate that love.

8. The Spirit's fullness is directly dependent on my confession of sin.

9. The Spirit's infilling makes me neither immune to sin nor free from temptation.

10. Being filled with the Spirit makes me much more sensitive to sin. In thus seeing my true status, the initial euphoria may be dampened, but the end result is true joy through confession.

11. God uses mountaintop experiences to stimulate further longings, even much later in life.

12. We must not depend on such experiences for our growth as Christians, but when God grants them, each crisis must be followed by a process.

Thinking It Through

Experience is the best teacher, but a hard one. It gives us the test before it teaches us the lesson. Did you learn useful lessons from your last crisis—whether it was good or bad? And how recently has God broken into your life, surprising you with joy?

Planting It Deep

" 'Do not come any closer,' God said [to Moses]. 'Take off your sandals, for the place where you are standing is holy ground.' . . . At this, Moses hid his face, for he was afraid to look at God." (Exodus 3:5-6)

"When Jacob awoke from his sleep, he thought, 'Surely the LORD is in this place, and I was not aware of it. . . . How awesome is this place! This is none other than the house of God; this is the gate of heaven.' " (Genesis 28:16-17)

Praying It In

O Lord,
having known the ecstasy
of special experiences,
I fear I shall try to live
from mountaintop
to mountaintop.
While asking You
to deliver me from that,
I also ask
that I may not fall
into the opposite trap.
May I never be satisfied
with the joyless existence
and the boring monotony
of mere religious routine.
Keep me balanced, Lord.
Amen.

I've Got My Priorities Straight

16

*"Because your love is better than life,
my lips will glorify you." (Psalm 63:3)*

The psalmist now moves to his second reason for thirsting after God—priorities! The beginning of the third millennium A.D. finds us with more of them than ever before. We are constantly sorting out what is priority and what is not.

A friend in England was the sole typist for five bosses. Almost every job she was given was marked "priority." Everyone wanted his work yesterday and she was supposed to please them all. When she threatened to quit, they reluctantly agreed she needed just one boss. From then on, that person alone determined the priority.

Thirty years ago, as the pace of life increased, a string of articles appeared, warning us of "the tyranny of the urgent." The important was being bypassed. True, there were priorities in both categories, but those in the "urgent" slot increasingly won the day. Time was becoming our ruthless master!

In our thirst after God we are mainly concerned with the "important" category. To cultivate this, we simply must learn to *make* time.

There used to be more general agreement on how to determine what is important. There was a body of truth we rightly considered absolute and unchanging. We need not read polls or surveys to conclude that a large segment of society no longer believes in absolute truth. Our mantra is "my view is as good as yours." Having thrown overboard the standards which kept society on course for millennia, we are now like an ocean liner without compass, map or anchor.

If we think there actually are right answers, we imply someone else is wrong, and that is unpardonable! Our national religion, "tolerance," drives home the point relentlessly. The one in the spotlight today is not the answer-giver but the question-asker! Questions are in! Answers are out! At least it stopped the arguments on what was important. Now everyone can be right! We each make up our own mind and that is supposed to be the end of it.

Such moral anarchy prevailed even in religious Israel before Samuel's day. Judges 17:6 tells us "every man did that which was right in his own eyes" (KJV).

Thinking in such increasingly blurry philosophical circles brings bondage, not freedom. It will get us nowhere fast! For, despite the popularity of the ideology, each of us has but one life—with no reruns! It is of paramount importance that we live that life not by half-truth but by "true-truth." Jesus (considered even by His enemies to have been a great teacher) unequivocally affirmed that God's truth, the Bible, was absolute truth—for all peoples, at all times.

That Bible clearly teaches that following this short span on earth we shall each stand before God to be judged by His priorities, not ours. Therefore the priority of all priorities must surely be that we determine what God considers important, so we can live by it and face Him on that coming day.

The writer of our text (Psalm 63:3) is a man after God's heart (and, I must add, after mine!). He has long ago made up his mind. He knows why he is on earth. His priorities are right. With all the demands upon him as king of a conquering nation, he nevertheless states in no uncertain terms the number-one priority in his life. "Your loving-kindness is better than life!" Because he is sure this is what God wants, he is determined to pursue it. Are we?

Thinking It Through

Have you sat down recently and written out your priorities in life? Are you living for those things which will be snatched from you at death? Or for that which will enrich your eternal relationship with God, and leave footprints to guide the next generation into the right paths?

Planting It Deep

"So we fix our eyes not on what is seen, but on what is unseen. For what is seen is temporary, but what is unseen is eternal." (2 Corinthians 4:18)

Praying It In

O Lord,
I get so hooked
on the things which are seen—
even physical life itself!
Deep down I want
to change my focus.
I want to put eternal realities
in the center of my gaze.
But I am so weak;
I keep falling back
into my old ways.
Give me, I pray,
a fresh vision of You,
and teach me to number my days
that I may apply my heart
unto wisdom.
Amen.

YOUR LOVE IS BETTER THAN LIFE

17

*"Because your love is better than life,
my lips will glorify you." (Psalm 63:3)*

We have thought on *our* priorities. Let's now think about David's. "God's love," he says, "is more important than life!"

With all his hardships (2 Samuel 15-17) I am amazed David could still focus on God's goodness at all. We'd likely grumble, complain and question God. Not so King David. "Your love is better than life!"

This word for "love" (mercy, faithfulness, fidelity or loyal-love) is God's foremost quality toward His people. The KJV's "Your *lovingkindness* is better than life," is somewhat archaic but a quite accurate translation.

He is saying, "The lasting things of your kingdom are more important than the fleeting things of mine—even life itself! When we put eternal values before temporal ones, we too will long after God."

Our everyday choices are the best indication of our priorities. How we use our time or money, the books we read, the topics we talk or think about. All these help us see what our life-principle really is; that one factor which most influences our decision-making.

It bothers me when I see how much mixed motivation I have! But God detects the deepest longing of our hearts. Though I so often fail, He is fully aware that my bottom line is "that I may know Him!" My deciding factor usually is, "Will this help me walk closely with the Lord?"

A schoolgirl who was asked to explain the difference between science and religion replied, "Science is material, but religion is immaterial." The use of her words (in medieval times) meant that science had to do with matter, whereas religion was about that which was not matter ("immaterial" meant "non-material"). But what at first *"was* not matter," later *"did* not matter"! "Immaterial" then came to mean "not pertinent to the matter in hand" and later still, "of no essential consequence; unimportant."

"Immaterial," as currently used, sends the message that eternal things, the only things which go on after the "wrap-up," are of no importance! What an upside down view of life!

King David would have had little patience with such linguistic gymnastics. He came to the right conclusion and nobody was going to rob him of it. For verse 3 anticipates St. Paul's "we fix our eyes not on what is seen, but on what is unseen. For what is seen is temporary, but what is unseen is eternal" (2 Corinthians 4:18).

In one of Europe's cathedrals there are three archways. Chiseled into the stone over the left archway is a rose, with the inscription, "That which pleases is but for a moment." Over the right archway is a cross, with the inscription, "That which troubles is but for a moment." The center archway has no symbol, just this inscription: "Only that which is unseen is eternal."

The New Testament confirms the three most lasting qualities are "faith, hope and love," then adding, "the greatest of these is love" (1 Corinthians 13:13). It's true, Lord! "Your love is better than life!"

If we value the eternal over the temporal, we will be able to say, "Though he slay me, yet will I trust in him" (Job 13:15, KJV). And if, like Paul, we were called on to stand before the Ephesian elders and say, "I know that none of you . . . will ever see me again," then we too could add: "I consider my life worth nothing to me." Both of these servants had one consuming passion—to know God and accomplish the task for which he had put them on earth. O God, give us that passion!

One day we will no longer have a choice between the things of God and the things of this life. Those who choose wisely now will come out far ahead of those who will later find themselves kicking and screaming as they are dragged away from their "toys," with no time to think anything through.

David had his priorities straight. Is it any wonder he was desperate for God! So it will be for us!

Thinking It Through

It is one thing to say you know that the eternal is more important than the temporal, but quite another to live it! List the ways in which most days of your life show you really believe it! You just may be surprised!

Planting It Deep

"Show me, O LORD, my life's end
and the number of my days;

78

let me know how fleeting is my life.
You have made my days a mere handbreadth;
*   the span of my years is as nothing before you.*
Each man's life is but a breath.

Man is a mere phantom as he goes to and fro:
*   He bustles about, but only in vain;*
*   he heaps up wealth, not knowing who will get it.*

'But now, Lord, what do I look for?
*   My hope is in you!' " (Psalm 39:4-7)*

Praying It In

O Lord,
I can be such a hypocrite;
one moment, in church,
saying one thing,
and the next, at home,
doing the very opposite!
You know, Lord,
where I confess
my priorities to be.
The trouble is
my life does not back up
my so-called beliefs.
Pull me up, Lord.
Keep bugging me
about the discrepancies
between what I say
and what I am.
Amen!

I'M COMMITTED, NO MATTER WHAT!

18

*"I will praise you as long as I live, and in your name
I will lift up my hands." (Psalm 63:4)*

"How foolish," some would say of David's third reason for thirsting, "to tell God you will praise Him as long as you live. How do you know He won't bring trouble into your life? Or fill the cup with something bitter? Who would want to praise Him then?"

"I would!" cries David. Yet he is no masochist; it is simply that he knows his God!

Life is made up of contrasts. Black and white, darkness and light, night and day. One of God's miracles is to keep them in balance, for, on earth, both parts of each pair have a key role to play.

The writer of Solomon's song well understood this principle of life and growth. He says, "Awake, north wind, and come, south wind! Blow on my garden, that its fragrance may spread abroad" (Song of Songs 4:16). It takes both the balmy breezes from the south and also the icy blasts from the north to produce fragrant gardens, strong trees and choice fruits.

When David commits himself (and he seems to say "no matter what"), he is acknowledging that what God chooses for his life is the best he could want. He may not enjoy the biting winds of winter any more than we. But he knows they are necessary to produce fragrance and fruit. It was the saintly Samuel Rutherford who said, "Grace grows best in winter."

It is a struggle for us to come to such healthy attitudes about what God allows in our lives. But it is essential we cultivate them. For we shall never get close to the heart of God without trouble of one kind or another. My thirst after God, if expressed in David's words in verse 1, almost invites the very adversity which will draw me close.

Affliction is a great watershed. It either drives us *to* God or *from* Him. Which course we take likely depends more on our existing relationship with God than any other factor.

I have come to the strong conviction that my closeness to God is more precisely measured by my capacity for suffering than it is by my capacity for joy. David knew this; yet he also knew that his God would always know how to strike the balance.

When things do not go our way, we find it hard to see God in them. But when they are to our liking, we have little difficulty seeing Him in our plans.

I recall my mother-in-law once showing me from John 21 that, after Jesus' death and resurrection, the disciples did not recognize Him on the shore at Capernaum. They had had a fruitless night fishing. The catch was zero. And who can see God in that? But then "the stranger" called to them suggesting where they should cast the net. With nothing to lose, they obeyed, still not knowing who He was. The result was amazing! The catch was so heavy they were unable to haul it in. And their immediate reaction? Of course. "It is the Lord!" (John 21:3-7).

Occasionally someone may say to me words like, "God was good to me yesterday." Tongue in cheek, I often reply, "Oh, wasn't He good the day before?" The point is made not only for their benefit, but for mine too. I need frequent reminding. It helps to cultivate an attitude of being "committed—no matter what!"

Thinking It Through

We need to ask ourselves frequently, "Do we ever ditch in the darkness what we learned in the light?" We must start laying down spiritual absolutes—attitudes and actions we will insist on putting into effect, especially when we do not feel inclined. (I have many such lists. They have been a most useful guide, particularly in a crisis!) Try it out!

Planting It Deep

"I will come to your temple with burnt offerings
and fulfill my vows to you—
vows my lips promised and my mouth spoke
when I was in trouble." (Psalm 66:13-14)

Praying It In

O Lord,
I thank You
that You are always good.
Sometimes I recognize it,
like now,
and sometimes I don't.
But I want to affirm, Lord,
that whether I recognize it
or not,
You are indeed always good!
And I thank You.
Amen!

LIFTING UP HOLY HANDS

19

"In your name I will lift up my hands." (Psalm 63:4)

Lips, hands and mouth! All three couplets in verses 3-5 mention a part of the human body. The lips glorify God (63:3); the hands are raised (63:4); the mouth praises (63:5).

We must not imagine our disembodied lips drifting upwards like a helium-filled balloon, while we sit watching them praise God. Nor do hands or mouth go off and do their own thing! David is not suggesting dismemberment. Nor is he endorsing the hypocrisy where I say something with my lips or do something with my hands that does not come from my heart.

This is the rather common biblical practice of using a part—here, part of the body—to represent the whole. Because the lips articulate praise, they are used to represent my entire being—body, soul and spirit. In John 17:1, Jesus "lifted up his eyes" (KJV) to heaven. His eyes represent His whole being focusing upon God. We call such a figure of speech a synecdoche.

David is saying that because God's love is better than life, his whole being will glorify God. While verbal praise comes through his lips, his whole body will be saying a hearty Amen!

The same principle applies as we extend our consideration of verse 4 (David's third reason for thirsting). Because of the more common practice of raising the hands in recent years, some observations may be helpful.

David's commitment-no-matter-what is now expressed physically. To "lift up my hands" to God means to lift up my whole being to Him. My hands represent my all. This is not just the style of certain ecclesiastical traditions. It is thoroughly biblical, mentioned at least a half-dozen times in Scripture. That is certainly more than closing our eyes when we pray (a good practice, but not a particularly biblical habit)!

When we pray lifting up our hands, we rededicate ourselves to God. In another psalm (143:6), David tells God, "I spread out my hands to you; my soul thirsts for you like a parched land." That idea of longing and aspiration would doubtless be in his mind here. But in 63:4, his primary motivation is to express undying praise to this always-good God for who He is and what He has done. This seems to be the most frequent reason for the raising of hands in the Bible, as it is also today in many churches.

The idea of moral purity is also conveyed, but the "holy" in "lift up holy hands" (1 Timothy 2:8) is not the usual word for "holy." It here means something done with devotion and piety, and therefore pleasing to God.

But it is "in your name" that David lifts up his hands. "God's name" is a biblical way of saying God's character—loving and just, holy and longsuffering, merciful and mighty, all in perfect balance. Because of David's confidence in God's unchanging character, he lifts up his hands in praise.

Like David, some of us have a more outwardly expressive way of conveying our inward feelings. Our generation has more liberty in this respect than the last. This is particularly true of the raising of hands, commonly seen today. Those conditioned to be more "dignified" in church often feel uncomfortable with this display of worship, and we should be sensitive to their feelings. But they, in turn, must be careful not to think of this worship as "exhibitionistic."

When King David outwardly expressed his joy at the return of the ark to Jerusalem in Second Samuel, we read that he and "the whole house of Israel were celebrating with all their might before the LORD" (6:5). His wife Michal "despised him in her heart" (6:16). When she reprimanded him, he said, "I *will* celebrate before the LORD" (6:21, emphasis added) and insisted that was more important than being traditionally dignified in his joy.

We need to ask God to give us that humility and reverence which will enable us to see ourselves as we really are and see Him as He really is. This will leave little room to be questioning other people's ways of worshiping God and will bring more pleasure to God's heart.

Thinking It Through

During worship, do you focus more on God or on the way others worship? Where the Spirit of the Lord is, there is liberty. And to lift up our hands if we are so inclined is most biblical indeed. Are you more influenced by your culture or church tradition than you are by the Bible? Do you need to be more tolerant of those who express themselves differently—whether they do or don't lift up their hands in worship?

Planting It Deep

"Ezra praised the LORD, the great God; and all the people lifted their hands and responded, 'Amen! Amen!' Then they bowed down and worshiped the LORD with their faces to the ground." (Nehemiah 8:6)

"I want men everywhere to lift up holy hands in prayer, without anger or disputing." (1 Timothy 2:8)

Praying It In

O Lord,
I thank You
for giving me
a reason to worship You.
Deliver me from
a critical spirit;
help me look at You
rather than looking at others;
let me never use
outward forms
as touchstones
to determine who is "spiritual"
and who is not.
Give me a sincere heart
to worship You, O Lord,
my Strength and my Redeemer.
Amen.

I'M ON THE TIPTOE OF EXPECTANCY

20

"My soul will be satisfied as with the richest of foods."
(Psalm 63:5)

As I write from a boat-house in an isolated cove on Vancouver Island, a heron has just settled on a flat rock, gradually being submerged by the incoming tide. With interminable patience he waits for a fish to come within grabbing distance.

It's been nearly twenty minutes already. I suspect the reason he keeps on waiting is that he has done this before. Each time his patience has been rewarded. He knows eventually he will get his meal. And so he waits—with his mouth watering.

That's the picture David paints. "My soul will be satisfied as with the richest of foods" (63:5). Like the heron, he knows God will satisfy the longing heart. He can almost taste his fish! And this is his fourth reason for thirsting after God.

Knowing that fellowship is possible is not as motivating as knowing it's around the next corner. When, like David, I'm on the tiptoe of expectancy, my mouth will be watering like Pavlov's dogs! In his imagination, David is already sitting down at the table.

With my being away frequently, Rosemary often invites friends for dinner the day after I return. Preparation usually starts the day before. What a welcome- home smell! A pervading sense of anticipation takes over. Breakfast and lunch next day are minimal, reluctantly eaten so the good won't interfere with the best.

With table attractively set, candles lit and music playing, the guests arrive. The courses come in conventional sequence—appetizers, followed by the grand entrance of the entree. Perhaps it is roast beef and Yorkshire pudding, garnished with all the eye desires. By this time, I am looking for a discreet way to loosen my belt. I succeed, but minutes later, I unwisely succumb to seconds.

The fellowship gets richer, the conversation more stimulating. The choices for dessert sound equally scrumptious. Tropical fruit with cream, strawberry-rhubarb crumble a la mode, or mouth-watering ice cream pie. I venture a simple "thank you" and find myself given a portion of each.

Opening my belt to the last notch, I push my bulging body back from the invading table. The second pot of coffee has finished brewing and the refill is the cue for an even more in-depth conversation. Engrossed in fellowship, nobody notices the music has stopped, the candles burned down and the calories are taking their toll. What a picture of all-absorbing fellowship!

That is the scene David is painting for us in verse 5. And the NIV's future tense translation puts it all into a mood of anticipation. He compares the feeding of his soul to a rich meal. In the same way as the delectable food has whetted the appetite and satisfied it to saturation point, he awaits the indescribable feast with the Lover of his soul. His inner man will be fed until he cries, "Stay your hand, Lord, I've got spiritual indigestion!"

Not all my encounters reach those heights, but the potential is there whenever I set the stage. I give God permission to invade the hidden parts of my life.

But the second line (another synecdoche) reminds me that the satisfaction of soul described here is not so I will become lazy and lethargic. We are not meant to live all our lives in the cloister, getting fat on God's richest foods. He expects us to return the upward blessing of praise and the outward blessing of loving service to others.

Can you remember when joyous anticipation characterized your mornings as you approached the Word and the Throne? To be reminded of those days when that sense of longing has all but disappeared gives us inward pain, but it also makes us conscious of our need for restoration.

Thinking It Through

There is something about the feel of a leather-bound Bible which like the smell of a dinner, sends the juices flowing within me. It's probably just conditioning, but I always get excited when I hold one in my hand. Because my experience of reading God's Word has always been a pleasant one, my sense of anticipation expands to fill my being. What is it in your life that excites you the most?

Planting It Deep

"Blessed are those whose strength is in you,
  who have set their hearts on pilgrimage. . . .
Better is one day in your courts
  than a thousand elsewhere.
I would rather be a doorkeeper in the house of my God
  than dwell in the tents of the wicked."
    (Psalm 84:5, 10)

Praying It In

O Lord,
I do recall
the early days
of my Christian life.
There was
a joy in my heart,
a smile on my face
and a spring in my step.
Where is the blessedness
I knew
when first
I met You, Lord?
Give me again
that sense of anticipation
as I open Your Word
and prepare my heart
to worship You.
Amen.

HAVE YOU MADE
THE PSALM YOUR OWN?

I t is essential, before going on in this wonderful psalm, that we start to apply it to our own lives. Otherwise we shall fall into a habit of reading, feasting and storing information in our heads without applying it to our hearts.

Having reached the end of the first of the three sections into which we divided the psalm, some suggestions may help us recall the steps to kindling a thirst after God.

Would the words of 63:1 be true of my life?

> O God, you are my God,
> earnestly I seek you;
> my soul thirsts for you,
> my body longs for you,
> in a dry and weary land
> where there is no water.

Am I really devoted to God? Am I diligent in my longing to know Him better? Am I desperate in my desire to see His face and feel His heartbeat? Am I truly addicted to God?

I may long to be like that, but sense I am a million miles from it. Am I willing to build dynamic incentives into my life to enable me to cultivate this thirst? If so, then the next four verses (2-5) will help me do that:

1. I must ask myself, "Where is the blessedness I knew when first I saw the Lord?" When or where was the highest peak in my experience with God? If I have lived on a higher plane, then I will be aware that a deeper and more meaningful relationship with God is possible (63:2). If I am a new Christian, or have never had any such mountaintop experience, I could start at the next verse.

2. I must determine what I consider the most important areas of life (63:3) If my earthly life were to suddenly end today, would God see that I valued eternal things more than the passing things of time? Am I willing from here on to give those matters priority wherever there is a clash?

3. I must get to know God better, by acquiring a deeper understanding of His character from the Bible. Does it tell me, in particular, that He is always good, whether I recognize it or not? If the Bible is clear that He is, am I willing, like David (63:4) to make a lifelong commitment to Him, no matter what He brings into my life?

4. I must persevere in having quality time alone with God each day. The joyous memories of yesterday's rendezvous with Him will increasingly excite me as I anticipate today's (63:5). Will I really persevere until the language of this verse becomes mine?

Note: It is good to recap! It recaptures the thoughts which may have passed through our minds as we were reading, and may otherwise have been lost. The four statements above sum up the four verses (2-5) we have just meditated on. Those verses will then become more meaningful to us, and likely stay with us.

A Prayer

O God, You are my God!
All You have been
to the psalmist,
to the patriarchs
and to the prophets,
I know You will be to me.

I thank You for the confidence
that I can depend on You
in the changing circumstances
of my life.
How I need Your stability
in the days ahead.

Show Yourself to me today
with the freshness
of the morning tide.
Flow over the dry and blotchy sands
of my life,
wiping out the marks
of yesterday's defeats
and in Your grace
letting me start over.
Amen.

GOD, MY SOUL'S DELIGHT

On my bed I remember you;
I think of you through the watches of the night.
Because you are my help,
I sing in the shadow of your wings.
My soul clings to you;
your right hand upholds me.
(Psalm 63:6-8)

Perhaps David is lying outside a desert cave under the clear night sky. It is likely that the conditions in which he wrote the earlier verses have not changed at all. And yet his longing is at last rewarded. For God longs for us to experience victory not only by escape but also by patient endurance.

Having reminded himself of his priorities, he had in verse 5 anticipated a glorious time of feasting upon God ("my soul will be satisfied as with the richest of foods"). That anticipation was in reality an expression of his faith. Now, in this short paragraph, he has "got through" to God and his cup is full. His entire being—mind, emotions and will—are now positively engaged with God. He revels in his relationship and lets us in on his joy.

We should not forget where these verses come in the psalm. The final outcome in the closing verses is his confidence in God in warfare. You will recall that we thought of the kinds of problems we too would face, most of them not military. But whether our testing is one of health, finances, family relationships or sudden crisis, our psalm still applies. We too can know this confidence.

Once more though, we need to remind ourselves that the topic of this psalm is not unconfessed sin but adverse circumstances. Sin must of course always be confessed and forsaken, or God will not even hear us (read Psalm 66:18). But the theme of this passage is the confidence we can find in God when trouble has been thrust upon us; the things allowed by Him for the various purposes suggested by Scripture.

We shall face those situations with confidence (63:9-11) only as we delight in God (63:6-8). But that delight itself, we saw, grows out of hungering and thirsting after Him (63:1-5).

The nature of the delight expressed here can be summed up in three words, one for each verse: Thinking! Singing! Clinging!

Intellectually, his seeking after God now stirs his mind to *think* about Him (63:6). Emotionally, his praising God causes him to burst into *song* (63:7). Volitionally, his longing for God finds him *clinging* to Him in his hour of need (63:8).

Let us "milk" each verse in order. Thinking, singing and clinging. Indeed when my own thirst has been kindled in the ways suggested earlier in these pages, I have sensed and expressed delight in each of these three avenues of the soul—my mind, my emotions and my will.

THINKING!

21

*"On my bed I remember you; I think of you
through the watches of the night." (Psalm 63:6)*

David's longing has turned to delight. His cup is full! His delight is summed up in three words: Thinking, singing, clinging! Here we shall consider the first one.

Thinking! "On my bed I remember you; I think of you through the watches of the night" (63:6). What a great way to spend sleepless hours—communing with God! For David, delighting in God involves thinking about Him, not just momentarily, but "through the watches of the night."

This "man after God's heart" could not possibly keep thinking about Him without recalling the many times, as a shepherd, God had come to his rescue. At any minute now, that wolf Absalom could appear from around a rock. David's flock of followers would not be spared. Likely this is why David could not sleep. But he had learned to turn his cares into prayers. Underlying this was his lifelong habit of turning his mind toward the things of God.

Opportunities to Think about God

When you can't sleep. Can you remember being told when you couldn't sleep, "Don't count the sheep; talk to the Shepherd"?

Have you tried thinking about Him? It usually gets you talking to Him.

I often try meditating on one of the roles God plays in our lives—such as Shepherd or Father or Potter. Or I try contemplating His omnipotence, omniscience and omnipresence. I think of aspects of His love, justice and faithfulness. His sheer greatness overwhelms me.

Over the years this type of thinking has been of immense value. It stirs in me a deeper longing for God. Such habits expand our understanding, increase our faith, and instill in us a spirit of prayer. They cultivate our thirst. It also provides me with a never-ending source of illustrations for public speaking. And of course, it usually sends me back to sleep!

Television commercials. If you are a normal human and find too many TV commercials hard to take, mute the sound and try turning the ad into something spiritually profitable. If food, think about feeding on Christ: if something you wear, think of a Christian's clothing or armor; if it's for a mattress, think about resting on Christ or the Word. And so on. The Spirit of God will set fire to the fuel!

Waiting for an appointment. What do you read in a doctor's waiting room? Whatever's on the table? How easily we can waste time. Ever thought of carrying a pocket New Testament so you can "redeem the time"? I usually have a blank 3x5 card inside the back cover, so I can capture the thoughts I get. Be sure to close your eyes to shut out visual distractions so you can contemplate God, especially those aspects you've been reading or thinking about while waiting.

There is a tendency to link contemplation with the desert fathers or life in a monastery, the exclusive practice of those who wear rough-haired shirts and take vows of poverty. This wrongly limits the practice to special people in special places. Such longing must pervade all situations and activities. It must become our way of life, the background music to every-thing we do, whether doctor or patient, homemaker or busi-nesswoman, salesman or monk.

Yes, thinking of God "through the watches of the night" will not only be my soul's delight. It will also lead to right liv-ing.

Thinking It Through

Our minds matter to God. We are to reason together with Him, to let the mind of Christ be in us and control us, and to be renewed in the spirit of our minds. Is your faith based more upon hearsay, ritual, tradition or emotion? Why don't you list the ways you can develop your mind to become more of a thinking Christian?

Planting It Deep

"I will praise the LORD, who counsels me; even at night my heart instructs me." (Psalm 16:7)

*"I will instruct you and teach you in the way you should go. . . .
Do not be like the horse or the mule,
which have no understanding." (Psalm 32:8-9)*

Praying It In

O Lord,
thank You
for giving me
the capacity to think.
I confess
I have thought more
about the concerns
of daily life
than I have about You.
But I want to change that,
before my mind settles in a rut.
Would You create in me
a clean heart and a renewed mind?
As I mine the depths of Your Word,
help me uncover precious gems
which will transform my mind
and set me on the right road.
For the sake
of Your great glory I pray.
Amen.

Singing!

22

"Because you are my help, I sing in the shadow of your wings."
(Psalm 63:7)

Singing, particularly when I am alone, often expresses the joy in my heart. This second delight of David's comes from a renewed sense of confidence in God.

Sometimes, however, I will choose to sing when I feel low or discouraged. Singing of God's greatness is a wonderful way to inspire confidence during a storm. For truth is true whether we feel it or not! It helps focus my mind on what God *can* do rather than worrying about what I *cannot* do. I sense that this was David's reason for singing here in verse 7 of our psalm.

Because God is his help, David can shelter "in the shadow of His wings." Usually, the phrase "the shadow of your wings" tells us there is trouble around. For a chick, hiding in that spot spells the best protection possible in times of danger.

David, however, could go even further! He says, in effect, "Not only will I be there, but I will *sing* under those wings." Surely this kind of fearlessness is not that of someone cocky and self-sufficient, but of one who is humbly leaning upon God. Paul and Silas had similar confidence when they sang praises to God at midnight though bound by prison chains.

And what an amazing sequel there was to that event (see Acts 16:25-40).

These words spell out where we must go in trouble—to "the shadow of His wings." Once we are there, we start singing. This same David, in this same desert a few years before, had written a song (recorded as Psalm 57), some of the opening words of which have been a comfort to me on more than one occasion: "I will take refuge in the shadow of your wings until the disaster has passed."

The singing David has in mind here is not a mantra. Nor is it something merely to occupy the mind so as not to think of the problem. Both those would be purely psychological mechanisms which place no importance whatever on the One who is the Object of faith. Such is not the Christian way. It is because the words are true and biblical that the One of whom they speak imparts that confidence to us.

I strongly suspect it was because David had taken time to think of the character of God when his mind was free (as we saw in our last segment) that he can recall those truths and pin his faith in them when trouble comes. In this way, trouble drives us *to* God, not *from* Him.

Music, both instrumental and vocal, has played a larger part in the lives and worship of this generation than when I was young. Yet I do recall with a tremendous amount of joy and emotion hearing my godly mother sing at the kitchen sink. She had been ill for many years and was no longer hitting the right notes. But that did not matter when she wanted to praise her God. Many of the hymns she sang were about trusting in the dark. Her favorite was

> Sun of my soul, Thou Saviour dear,
> It is not night if Thou be near;
> Oh, may no earth-born cloud arise
> To hide Thee from Thy servant's eyes.[1]

She had proved her Savior after many bedridden years. Now she could look back to those years and draw strength from their memory. Like David, she too could say, "Because you are my help, I will sing in the shadow of your wings."

Thinking It Through

Because the Christian has much to be happy about, there is good reason for a song in his heart. Have you allowed the burdens of life to rob you of that song? When are you going to sing again as you move around the kitchen or laundry room or drive the car?

Planting It Deep

"Sing to the LORD a new song,
  for he has done marvelous things. . . .
Make music to the LORD with the harp,
  with the harp and the sound of singing."
    (Psalm 98:1, 5)

"Speak to one another with psalms, hymns and spiritual songs. Sing and make music in your heart to the Lord, always giving thanks to God the Father for everything in the name of our Lord Jesus Christ." (Ephesians 5:19-20)

Praying It In

O Lord,
there is just so much
to praise You for.
Thank You so much
for putting a new song
in my mouth,
"a hymn of praise
to our God."
I used to sing more, Lord.
Help me
to revive the practice,
that
daily
I will be
making melody in my heart
unto the King of kings.
I pray in the Name
of the One who put music
into our souls
in the first place.
Amen.

CLINGING!

23

*"My soul clings to you;
your right hand upholds me." (Psalm 63:8)*

David's third delight is "clinging." I often think of the late pastor Wang Ming Dao, China's most noted Christian prisoner, who, after twenty-three years in prison without Bible or hymnbook, said of Chinese Christians, "We have nothing—no pastors, no churches, no Bibles—nothing. We have only God! Therefore we go to Him in desperation!"

Such words make a further definition of clinging unnecessary.

Sometimes our minds are too fogged up to do the kind of thinking we saw in 63:6. Or again, trouble may be so severe that it is just too hard for us to try and sing, as in verse 7. But the sentiments of verse 8 may well become easier to practice in a time of trouble: "My soul clings to You."

The King James Version summed up the meaning of "clinging" even more correctly with "My soul followeth hard after thee."

"Following Hard after God" was one of the titles I had thought of for this book. Our thirsting after God will surely include following hard after Him.

The NIV's "clinging" is one of the colorful meanings of this Hebrew word. It is used of a man being united to or cleaving to his wife (Genesis 2:24) and in more than one place of the tongue cleaving to the roof of the mouth (see Psalm 137:6). The same word is used in the touching story of Ruth cleaving to Naomi in Ruth 1:14. It means to keep close to someone. It is in this context that we can see that the meaning carries also the thought of affection and loyalty.

Whereas a word usually means one thing in one context, it is my strong sense that there is no need to choose with this one. We must follow hard after God, keeping close to Him, and when we catch up, cling to him in affection, loyalty and dependence, never letting go.

The exhortation to cling will be particularly comforting to us when we are in troubling circumstances. It is in times like these, with our medical or financial Absaloms pursuing us, that we may be more inclined to pursue God.

This is less difficult when we have previously laid down spiritual and moral absolutes for a crisis. This habit is useful where Scripture urges us to adopt a certain attitude or course of action. As we saw earlier, I try to put those words into the form of an easy-to-remember principle, fixing it in my mind for use in times of trial. What you resolve to do beforehand can help you greatly when your reason is more clouded. Such plans can be filed in the mind's filing cabinet under "What to do if . . ." I have several "drawers" full of such "files"!

In a week or so I shall undergo surgery. Having been told which way I must move my body post-operatively, I am actually doing it now. What may be difficult to grasp when I am in pain is easier to learn when I have less.

A good example to try out this preparatory system would be our need for protection against making wrong decisions in a crisis. Second Chronicles 20:9 says, "If calamity comes upon us . . . we will stand in your presence . . . and will cry out to you in our distress, and you will hear us and save us." Why not try that now (write on a card for example, "If such-and-such happens, I will do this") and make it the first file in your cabinet? You could label this one "panic" or "calamity."

But the most reassuring part of Psalm 63:8 is the second line. For "my soul clings to you" is followed by "your right hand upholds me." What consolation! A friend suggested a helpful analogy: While I, the Rock climber, must cling to the Rock, it is the Rock—our great God Himself—who really holds me up. I may slip, but "underneath are the everlasting arms" of the One who says, "I'll never, no never, no never forsake!"

Satan may desire, as with Peter, to sift me like wheat. But my Intercessor will pray for me, so that my faith does not fail (Luke 22:31-32).

Thinking It Through

Can you recall times when your mind was so fogged up with trouble that you could not think straight? Or so preoccupied with worry that you had no song in your mouth? Your best plan at such times is simply to cling to God and His promises. An added bonus is having decided beforehand "what to do if . . ." It has been wisely observed that we do not live by God's answers, but by His promises!

Planting It Deep

"When you pass through the waters,
  I will be with you;
and when you pass through the rivers,
  they will not sweep over you.
When you walk through the fire,
  you will not be burned;
  the flames will not set you ablaze.
For I am the LORD, your God." (Isaiah 43:2-3)

Praying It In

O Lord,
I confess that
I often give the appearance
of being able to cope.
Little do my friends know
what You know—
how scared I sometimes am!
It has helped me to read
that this military strongman,
King David,
sometimes found it necessary
to hide
under the shadow of Your wings
or simply cling to You alone.
Give me too the courage
to admit my weakness;
For it is in my weakness
that I will find Your strength.
Amen!

MY SOUL'S CONFIDENCE

24

"But the king [the psalm's author]
will rejoice in God." (Psalm 63:11)

Thinking, singing, clinging (verses 6, 7, 8)! "I can just imagine myself sitting in a monastery garden," you say, "lost in wonder, love and praise," and listening to the birds! Who wouldn't feel close to God?

"Thinking? My mind would go down roads I have never thought about. *Singing?* Imagine taking a half of each hour singing praises to God. *Clinging?* How I would love to bask in God's sunshine, talking, loving and clinging.

"But that's fantasy land!" you say. "I have work to do. The kids must be dressed, the meals cooked. I must get to the plant on time. There's that unfinished job on the bench and that difficult report to do. I have no time to think and sing and cling. I'll leave that to monks and ministers!"

But how wrong you would be! For all three activities are to be my strong foundation as I go about my work. It's not work *or* God. It's *both!* It is these very verses which will make each workday fulfilling and enjoyable.

David, the author of our psalm and the king of verse 11, has come to that place of being positive in spirit and confident in God. So it will be with us!

For whether our daily activities involve people or projects, business or domestic, it is these attitudes of mind and emotion, fellowship and dependence which give us confidence. Our approach to the jobs we must tackle and the people we must rub shoulders with is transformed when we build on such delight.

Thinking about His kingdom will strengthen you with principles with which to live your life and do your work. The *singing* (though it may well be background music as you make melody in your heart, not disturbing others) will help you do your work with contentment. And "following hard" and *clinging* will help you see the importance of obeying your earthly "master," doing your work with integrity and giving a hundred cents to the dollar.

Do you feel cornered or trapped? Have your words been quoted out of context? Is there gossip? Whatever your difficulty, our great God understands the situation. Jesus was tested in all points that we are. Whatever the problem, this psalm applies. Except for unconfessed sin—which we must repent of!

The thirsting which led us to delight now leads us into a new confidence in this great God (63:9-11).

The language of the psalm shows David is seeking God's face, not just God's hand. He wants God Himself more than His handouts. It is when we are longing, thirsting, desperate to see Him for His own sake (as in 63:1-5), that we will cling to Him, leaning on His breast—feeling His heartbeat and enjoying His fellowship (63:6-8).

We dare not change the order. For only when we look at His face will we know whether we are comfortable asking Him to open His hand to grant our requests (63:9-11). We may see it is not in keeping with His will.

Our confidence in God may not result in a change of our circumstances. I doubt whether the facts changed from the beginning to the end of this psalm. The confidence of victory that David shows in the closing verses results from God's promises to him as Israel's anointed king. For God does not always promise to remove *our* burdens.

But one thing is sure! God will either remove the problem or give us the grace to bear it. We can be confident either way. For "underneath are the everlasting arms!" So follow hard after Him! Think! Sing! Cling! and be confident!

Thinking It Through

God gives the very best to those who leave the choice with Him. He alone knows whether your problem, or the removal of it, is best for your training as His child. Are you willing to trust Him—to tell Him you are confident that He will give victory either way? Remember that a cross, not a flower, is the symbol of our faith!

As we leave this beautiful morning psalm of the early church, why not set yourself a short-term goal of reading it through each morning before your daily reading?

Planting It Deep

"To keep me from becoming conceited because of these surpassingly great revelations, there was given me a

*thorn in my flesh, a messenger of Satan to torment me.
Three times I pleaded with the Lord to take it away from
me. But he said to me, 'My grace is sufficient for you, for
my power is made perfect in weakness' " (2 Corinthians
12:7-9).*

Praying It In

O Lord,
It's so hard being human!
There are so many problems
and I am always praying
that You will take them away.
Help me to see
that sometimes
You are kind enough
to let them remain.
I am learning
that the strength You then give
for me to persevere
is worth even more
in the long run
than getting rid of
the problem.
Keep on teaching me, Lord.
Amen.

A Prayer

Thank You, Lord
for preserving
this inspiring psalm,
giving me a window
to see into the heart
of Your servant David.

His words have expressed
the longings of my own heart,
and challenged me
to face up to
the shallowness
of my commitment to You.

But I confess that
while I have come before
to such crossroads
in my life,
I have often failed
to carry through
with the commitments I made.

Lord, I don't want that
to happen this time.
Will You prod me and nudge me
the moment I am
in danger of slipping?

Make me like David,
a person after Your own heart.
Give me an ever-deepening thirst,
a craving that is never satisfied.
And teach me
that my satisfaction
will come from the craving itself;
Because I know
that however well I get to know You
There will always be more of You
far beyond my meager comprehension.
Amen.

PART THREE

Pleading

Exodus 33:18–34:8, 29

18Then Moses said, "Now show me your glory."

19And the LORD said, "I will cause all my goodness to pass in front of you, and I will proclaim my name, the LORD, in your presence. I will have mercy on whom I will have mercy, and I will have compassion on whom I will have compassion. 20But," he said, "you cannot see my face, for no one may see me and live."

21Then the LORD said, "There is a place near me where you may stand on a rock. 22When my glory passes by, I will put you in a cleft in the rock and cover you with my hand until I have passed by. 23Then I will remove my hand and you will see my back; but my face must not be seen."

1The LORD said to Moses, "Chisel out two stone tablets like the first ones, and I will write on them the words that were on the first tablets, which you broke. 2Be ready in the morning, and then come up on Mount Sinai. Present yourself to me there on top of the mountain. 3No one is to come with you or be seen anywhere on the mountain; not even the flocks and herds may graze in front of the mountain."

4So Moses chiseled out two stone tablets like the first ones and went up Mount Sinai early in the morning, as the LORD had commanded him; and he carried the two stone tablets in his hands. 5Then the LORD came down in the cloud and stood there with him and proclaimed his name, the LORD. 6And he passed in front of Moses, proclaiming, "The LORD, the LORD, the compassionate and gracious God, slow to anger, abounding in love and faithfulness, 7maintaining love to thousands, and *forgiving wickedness, rebellion and sin. Yet he does not leave the guilty unpunished; he punishes the children and their children for the sin of the fathers to the third and fourth generation."*

⁸Moses bowed to the ground at once and worshiped.

And the result?

²⁹When Moses came down from Mount Sinai . . . he was not aware that his face was radiant because he had spoken with the LORD.

BACK ALLEY IN CHINA

25

"When Moses came down from Mount Sinai . . .
he was not aware that his face was radiant
because he had spoken with the LORD." (Exodus 34:29)

It was Sunday evening. It was getting dark, and my wife and I stood in a dimly lit alley in a large city in South China. We were trying to find where the Christians met. Two- and three-story buildings lined the lane, but there were few people we could ask for directions.

Thirty years had gone by since we had lived in Hong Kong, and my Chinese was very limited and rusty. I did try, but made little headway. It was difficult because of the secretive nature of what I wanted to know. How do you ask in a strange tongue where the Christians are meeting illegally?

Suddenly two women appeared almost out of nowhere. The younger tapped my arm, beckoning us to follow them. I assumed she knew someone who spoke English, but as I looked at her, the dim alley light struck the side of her face. As it did, I saw the glory of my King!

With new confidence, I enquired in a questioning Chinese tone, "Jesus?" Smiling warmly, she replied, "Jesus!" All doubt dissolved and we followed them down the alley to the house church. We climbed the stairs and, sitting on a bench, joined sixty Chinese believers as they prayed. Thanking God for this incredible privilege, we soon realized that an adjoining room, a stairway and a third room downstairs housed another 140. And that this was the third group to pack the house that day.

Most of these had suffered for their faith in Christ. Many had been in prison and, from what we understand, almost every family represented had at least one member who was incarcerated or being punished at that very time.

Thinking back over that evening, I was amazed that it all started with my seeing God in that radiant face there in the lane. That reflection was, at that moment, more trustworthy and reassuring than a stranger giving us clear directions or a map showing us the location of the house.

The glory of God is inevitably reflected in the faces and lives of those who spend much time with Him. It is surely this, even more than the ability to explain the great facts of the gospel, which is the telltale evidence of a vibrant faith and of close communion with God.

Quite early in my walk with God, I came across a most illuminating verse in Exodus 34: "When Moses came down from Mount Sinai with the two tablets of the Testimony in his hands, he was not aware that his face was radiant because he had spoken with the LORD" (34:29).

I was a new Christian and although I understood but little of the many lessons taught in that passage, I clearly recall the vivid impact that short verse had upon my thinking at that time. Now, half a century later, it is our privilege to look again at this most descriptive passage so we can all find help in establishing some regular habit of thinking about God and worshiping Him.

For as it was with Moses, so it will be with us. When we spend time alone with God, our lives will reflect His. This most rewarding of all encounters will then magnetically impact the lives of others and ultimately bring a willingness to listen to God's truth which leads to salvation. Yet it is likely that we too will be quite unaware of our influence!

Times of solitude and contemplating God are essential to our growth as Christians. Our thirsting after Him will stimulate this desire more than anything else. Without it, our service for God will become as burdensome as pushing a car without gas, or as futile as telling an empty glove to pick up a book. We will lack that power and glow which show the reality of our faith.

Thinking It Through

Does my Christian life and witness consist of only a quick decision years ago plus an occasional opening of my mouth? Do those I meet know that I am a follower of Jesus, whether I speak holy words or not? Both "presence and proclamation" are needed so that others can more fully understand, but there should be something most appealing about the way I look and listen, and how I react and conduct myself.

Planting It Deep

"Love must be sincere. Hate what is evil; cling to what is good. Be devoted to one another in brotherly love. Honor one another above yourselves. Never be lacking in zeal, but keep your spiritual fervor, serving the Lord. Be joyful in hope, patient in affliction, faithful in

prayer. Share with God's people who are in need. Practice hospitality." *(Romans 12:9-13)*

Praying It In

Lord, I often wonder
why it is
so few, if any,
can see You in me!
I love Your work,
I enjoy Your people
and I delight in Your Word!
But somehow,
something is missing!
Sometimes I wonder
could that "something"
be "Someone"?
I want to see You again Lord,
and feel You close to me.
I crave
that sense of Your presence,
not just so I'll feel good,
but so I'll grow more like You.
Then, by seeing me,
others will see You.
Oh, Lord,
give me a fresh glimpse
of Your glory!
It has been so long
and I am weary of waiting!
Amen.

GOD STIMULATES THE LONGING

26

STEP 1: "Now show me your glory." (Exodus 33:18)

We shall travel through these fourteen brief verses to trace the steps Moses took to see and reflect God's glory. These will prove invaluable as a guide to our "quiet time." I have selected seven "pegs" from our passage (Exodus 33:18-34:8) on which to hang some practical suggestions for cultivating this.

The Holy Spirit creates our thirst. But He expects us to cultivate it. We do that by drinking. Don't forget: spiritually, drinking makes us more thirsty, not less. We will understand this better as we proceed. The more of God's glory we see, the more we shall long for. It is a never-ending process "from glory to glory."

Indeed, that is the very word Moses uses when he makes his request. He says to God, "Now show me your glory" (33:18). What does he mean?

God's glory is His radiant splendor; anything and everything it is possible for me to know about God. It is all God deems expedient to show me. I just wonder how blinding would be the brilliant glory of what He chooses to conceal.

If even the rays of the sun (the only part God lets me see) possess the capacity to permanently damage the naked eye so that I must protect myself during an eclipse, how gracious of God to conceal the actual body of the sun, of which the rays are but the visible expression. The parallel with God's glory is clear.

The A.W. Tozer I knew had a deep, ongoing longing to see God's glory. He was never satisfied with what God had shown him yesterday. He always wanted more!

I am glad God did not answer Moses' request to see His glory with the put-down, "Hey, Moses, why are you so greedy? Don't you remember the day you saw the burning bush? [See Exodus 3.] How I spoke to you out of that bush and called you into ministry? Come on, Moses, you've already seen My glory! Why are you asking again?"

Moses certainly did remember that amazing encounter. How could he forget? That revelation of God must have fairly blown his mind. But the sight had only whetted Moses' appetite. It merely made him long for more. From that day he became "hooked"—on God!

Of course, as Christians we are fully satisfied with the finished work of Jesus on the cross 2,000 years ago. Yet it is equally true that we never seem to be satisfied with drinking from that Spring of Living Water. Why? How can it be that the more we drink the more thirsty we become?

We saw earlier that the immediate satisfaction from drinking is short-lived, because with each fresh installment, God increases our capacity. So no sooner are we satisfied than we become thirsty again. And this is healthy—it was meant to be so!

But we must never forget that Moses' longing was for God *Himself*. Many of us just have to learn from our own mistakes that we must never look for satisfaction from the peripheral things of God's kingdom. If we do, we shall finish up missing the Center Himself.

So if I long to have a life which reflects God's glory, I must learn to seriously cultivate my thirst for God. Cultivating means it is I who must take the next step, not merely wait around for God to zap me! Like Moses, I must express my longing to God and then get down to following His directions in the Bible on how to pursue it.

The nature of God and the Old Testament record of the ways He revealed Himself to humankind are surely among the most difficult to grasp, yet search-rewarding truths in all the Bible. I have tried to balance the using of my God-given mind and spirit with the recognition that there are some truths simply beyond my comprehension. In such matters, reasonable speculation must stop short of dogmatic conjecture, while still rejoicing that God became flesh and lived among us as Jesus.

I have gone into just a little more depth on this amazing theme in Rabbit Trail #1 at the back of the book. If you have grasped this chapter, you will find it worthwhile and mind-stretching to go to that rabbit trail before moving on.

Thinking It Through

How intense is your sense of yearning to know God better than you do—not just intellectually, but in your spirit too? Eternal life somehow does that to us! How we must grieve the Holy Spirit by not responding to His nudging when He longs to show us something. If He prompts you again while reading this book, will you say: "Speak, LORD, for your servant is listening" (1 Samuel 3:9)?

Planting It Deep

"I have much more to say to you, more than you can now bear. But when he, the Spirit of truth comes, he will guide you into all truth. He will not speak on his own; he will speak only what he hears, and he will tell you what is yet to come. He will bring glory to me by taking from what is mine and making it known to you." (John 16:12-14)

Praying It In

O Lord,
I am so slow to grasp
what You long for me to know.
Yet each time Your Holy Spirit
wants me to listen,
I am just too busy with things.
Give me a responsive spirit,
so that
when He next knocks
at my heart's door,
I will eagerly open it,
make Him feel at home
and listen to all
He wants to teach me
about Your glory.
Amen.

GOD DETERMINES THE PLACE

27

STEP 2: *"There is a place near me." (Exodus 33:21)*

In response to Moses' "Show me your glory," God now designates the place for an encounter which will be second to none in the Old Testament (33:19). "There is a place near me" (33:21) was a cleft in the rock on Sinai, possibly the very cave where Elijah met God on Mount Horeb.

Years ago, when I was in business in Britain, I chanced along an interesting country road in Somerset. There was a pie-shaped slice carved out of an unmarked cliff where Augustus Toplady had written a famous hymn. Into this "cleft in the rock" the traveler had scrambled when surprised by a sudden storm. As the elements beat upon the cliff, he found himself absolutely safe and dry, the full fury of the storm being borne by the rock.

It reminded him of two scriptures: "That rock was Christ" (1 Corinthians 10:4) and "You are my hiding place" (Psalm 32:7). As the storm beat upon the rock, he penned the words: "Rock of ages, cleft for me, let me hide myself in Thee." That hymn has brought untold blessing and comfort to many caught in the storms of life.

The place we can best see God's glory is the "cleft Rock" of Christ's body, when he died for us on Mount Calvary. This hymn speaks of "His riven side," for Jesus' side was "cleft" by a Roman spear; from it flowed His blood to cleanse from sin.

That spot is our hiding place (the "place near me"), sheltering us from God's wrath upon sin. I have safety and security when I hide in that cleft, for "payment God will not twice demand, first at my bleeding Surety's hand, and then again at mine." It will also shelter me from life's many storms.

Some of us also designate a place in our homes where we can spend time alone with God. But sometimes we have to make do. In such cases it is good to remember that "God . . . does not live in temples built by hands" (Acts 17:24). Although no more essential than a carving of Jesus is for prayer, if found, such a place is valued as "a place near Me."

Having lived in more than twenty homes in four countries, I have used many such places to meet with God. Also, being away often in ministry, I am used to finding a new spot almost daily. And whether in Australia or Alaska, the Andes or the Alps, Serbia or South Dakota, I can always find "a place."

Indoors or outdoors, facing glacial peaks or unadorned motel-room walls, I have sought to gaze upon God. I recall precious times in barns, fields, forests and—a favorite—perched atop an old wooden gate leading to a meadow. I find I am almost unaware of the "where I am" because the "why I'm here" takes over my spirit.

While living in Eastern Canada, I would enjoy sitting near the basement furnace, but not for the (often counterproductive) heat. Dr. Tozer urged me to seek quietness before comfort, and you may think the noise of an oil-burning furnace is anything but. Yet it was that very factor which served the purpose admirably. The loud, consistent sound effectively smothered the distracting noises of talking, laying of tables or creaking of floor-boards. I could focus on God alone.

On the 100-plus days I spend home each year, I sit on the floor leaning against a sofa. An odd place? No! It not only suits my arthritic condition but also tends to keep me awake. And when I sit there, I know why! I am conditioned to expect that God will "come through." Of course, God often breaks through in the everyday routines of life. So while not limiting Him, I still "set the stage" the best I know how.

"Don't call it your office, young man. It's your study! You probably won't expect God to speak to you in an office." I can hear Tozer now. His point is well taken—expectancy through conditioning. I try to follow it when getting alone, but bear in mind too that familiarity can breed contempt.

Thinking It Through

Long before telephones or e-mail, God perfected a way to be accessible to all. He's never too busy, "out of the office" or "in a meeting." When you want to see His glory, He is ready waiting. Do you use this privilege? Reading Rabbit Trail #1 will help you to that end.

Planting It Deep

"Above the expanse over their heads was what looked like a throne of sapphire, and high above on the throne was a figure like that of a man . . . and brilliant light surrounded him. Like the appearance of a rainbow in the clouds on a rainy day, so was the radiance around

him. This was the appearance of the likeness of the glory of the LORD. When I saw it, I fell facedown."
(Ezekiel 1:26-28)

Praying It In

O Lord,
I've missed
so many opportunities
to get to know You.
I confess
I've been more involved
in less important things.
But I want to start over!
So I boldly ask,
"Show me Your Glory."
You have every right
to delay, like I did,
but I ask
that in Your grace
despite my procrastination,
You will show me Yourself
in increasing measure.
Amen.

GOD SUGGESTS THE TIME

28

STEP 3: "Be ready in the morning." (Exodus 34:2)

Although the morning is my personal choice, here again, just as there is no place where God's voice cannot be heard, there is no time that He will not speak. I am reminded of how often the psalmist heard God's voice in "the night watches."

Becoming a Christian at twenty while living in Hong Kong, I was soon spending many hours in the Word—often from 10 p.m. till 2 a.m.—seeking wisdom to live. I was a night person! It was my best time. Now, nearly fifty years later, I am neither a night nor a morning person. I'm dropping off to sleep at 10:30, and next morning often don't feel like getting up at all, let alone early.

But as with most things in life, what *feels* good is not usually what *is* good—in the long run! God is more interested in our holiness than in our happiness. Because ultimately only holiness can bring happiness, then only what *is* good will finally *feel* good! So I have chosen to force myself out of bed early most mornings. Notice verse 4 goes further, adding "early."

Staying in the home of a Yugoslavian pastor living in Vienna, I learned that he had a fixed time schedule that worked well. Following breakfast, he would return to his bedroom from 8 to 10:30 each morning. Having had a quiet time, this would be a period of intercession. He would imagine his bedroom floor was a map of Yugoslavia and would move around it on his knees. "Arriving" at each city, he would intercede for those pastors. His place and time were consistent. God certainly "enlarged his coasts."

My wife Rosemary seems more flexible in both time and place than I. She can work her time schedule around either my ministry engagements or the needs of others in our home. She will determine her "place" (usually family room, kitchen table or bedroom) depending on overnight guests or whether before or after breakfast. She simply must have her forty-five minutes or so each morning with God. Her wonderful serving spirit is kept buoyant only because she insists on so drawing her strength from the Lord.

It would be wrong to require everyone to toe the morning line. Some, particularly mothers of young children, often find mornings the most difficult time. (See Rabbit Trail #4, an article my wife wrote when our children were young.)

Years ago, while preaching in the southern States, I was invited to a young couple's home for dinner. In their early twenties, they had been married only thirteen months, but had two-month old twin boys.

The husband was in the military and, both being from New England, they were far from "home." The young mother wanted so much to get to know God but life wasn't easy. In one twelve-month period she had had too many changes—new city, new church, new home, new husband and new babies.

The twins were on "shift-work." Often up throughout the night, she would drop off to sleep when she tried to have a time with the Lord. She found a way out. She bought four inexpensive paperback New Testaments and broke the bindings so they would stay open. She put one on the kitchen counter, one in the bathroom, one beside her bed and one on the babies' changing table. She would grab several two- or three- minute slots with the Lord in the Word as she went about her daily chores. Where there's a will, there's a way!

Thinking It Through

How time runs away with us! We rarely "find time" for God; we just have to "make time." That means planning. If the mother of those twins could find a way to plan the important, surely I can! What routines would I have to change to make this a daily habit? Good time to read Rabbit Trail #4.

Planting It Deep

"Let the morning bring me word of your unfailing love,
*   for I have put my trust in you.*
Show me the way I should go,
*   for to you I lift up my soul." (Psalm 143:8)*

Praying It In

O Lord,
I always have time
to do
what I think is important,
but mostly
I shortchange You.
Teach me to plan
so that the urgent
no longer conquers
the important.
For one day,
sooner than I may think,
the important
will become urgent!
Give me the wisdom
and give me the will
to put first things first.
Amen.

GOD ORDERS THE PRESENTING

29

STEP 4: "Present yourself to me there." (Exodus 34:2)

Presenting myself to meet a high-ranking dignitary takes preparation. How much more so for a king! Like Moses, I am now about to enter the presence of the King of all kings! How do I prepare?

In the earthly realm I may think about my dress. In the spiritual realm I must think of the condition of my heart. I need the posture of one privileged to be presented to the King by my Savior. This suggests I come with two attitudes:

First, I must present myself in an attitude of *confession*—asking for God's forgiveness. I will be very thankful that the throne is one of grace! I will be conscious of the greatness and majesty of the One who sits upon it. I will also be aware of my own smallness, at His feet.

I will take off my shoes, figuratively speaking, for like Moses at the bush, the place on which I stand is holy ground. I will come with reverence and humility. Such an attitude of spirit will bring a deep consciousness of my sin, so that—again like Moses—I will want to hide my face, "afraid to look upon God." This, but for the grace of God, I would have to do.

Here, of course, is the place where true communion starts. I will find that, with God and men, fellowship begins at my points of weakness, not my points of strength. As I present myself, I will show my willingness to come clean and expose my sin. This is the place of repentance, of contrition and often of tears.

From such brokenness, wholeness will come—it is one of the many paradoxes of the kingdom. The Holy Spirit will point me to the cross, where Jesus bore all God's judgment on my sin. The Son of God thus becomes refreshingly precious to me each time I am pronounced forgiven.

If I come before God in the right spirit, I need very little stimulus to trigger confession. I can then spend much of this time of communion in other forms of prayer.

Either spontaneous or set forms can be equally fresh, particularly when I have become too accustomed to the other. When my spirit is just not on the right wavelength, I read Psalm 51 or 32, or perhaps the sufferings of Jesus on the cross. These very soon bring me to the point of confession.

Secondly, I must present myself in an attitude of *consecration*. I must submit to God's direction. Are my mind and spirit open to what He will show me as we commune? Do I have a readiness to go, freshly empowered, to do His bidding that day? Having presented my body as a living sacrifice to Him, I will then be able to discover and approve—the double meaning of that Romans 12:2 verb—what is that "good, and acceptable, and perfect, will of God" (KJV).

Perhaps I have already broadly discovered His will in a certain matter. Maybe His Spirit has directed and nudged me while reading His Word. And while there will be other confirming factors, nothing God shows me will ever go against the clear teaching of His Word. In this way I will learn over time how to discern the voice of the Spirit, amidst the cacophony of sounds competing for my attention that day.

Both of these aspects of "presenting myself" are crucial. The first, *confession*, clears the lines from the static of sin, so I will hear when God speaks; the second, *consecration*, expresses my willingness to listen to His direction for the day.

I can therefore stand with confidence at this fork in the road of life. Looking back, I will see the word "forgiven" written by God over all the wrong turns I ever made. Looking forward, I know with increasing assurance which of the two roads I must take to get where He wants me to be. Forgiveness for the past; guidance for the future. What more could I want as I present myself to His Majesty?

Thinking It Through

Planning is good, when it guards me from drifting and wasting time. But it can be bad if I am more eager to plan my own day than to consult with God. He usually works two ways: He uses my renewed mind so I will plan wisely but will often break in with His "interruptions." Blessed interruptions! May I be open to His voice!

Planting It Deep

"Whether you turn to the right or to the left, your ears will hear a voice behind you, saying, 'This is the way; walk in it.' " (Isaiah 30:21)

Praying It In

O Lord,
How I need
to present myself to You
more often—
especially in confession!
I let my sins mount up,
when I should be keeping
short accounts with You.
Right now, for instance,
I need to confess
my proneness
to plan my day
my way!
I am Your servant, Lord,
and I need to consult You
more frequently.
Teach me
to come,
to listen
and to obey.
Amen.

GOD INSISTS ON THE SOLITUDE

30

STEP 5: *"No one is to come with you." (Exodus 34:3)*

ooking back through half a century of knowing God,
there is no doubt my most memorable times were when I
was alone with Him. Yet I have no plans to run off and join a
hermitage, for I strongly believe in the Church. Corporate
worship brings joy and bonding, with God and with others.

Like two wings of a bird, personal and corporate worship
safeguard each other. It was Dietrich Bonhoeffer who said,
"Let him who cannot be alone beware of community. Let him
who is not in community beware of being alone."[1]

Some years ago, emerging from seven days' silent retreat in
a Franciscan monastery in rural England, I recall telling one of
the brothers how spiritually encouraged I was to think I had
not sinned with my tongue for a whole week. He quickly cau-
tioned me.

He had been a BBC producer and had pondered similar
thoughts during his early days as a friar. "Sharing our
thoughts," he said, "encourages correction if we are wrong.
And while we may not sin with the tongue in silent retreat,
unworthy or uncorrected thoughts have a greater opportunity
to deepen their roots."

I must admit I was rather stunned. I was certainly brought down a peg or two from my "holy hill." But his observation surely confirmed Bonhoeffer's. We need the corporate to balance the personal. And if I am conscious of a sinning tongue, I need to remember that the answer to abuse is not *no* use but *correct* use (read David in Psalm 39:1-3).

Yet, like me, your worship may be more inhibited in a group than when alone. We all need times when we are not embarrassed to take off our masks. This is why God says to Moses, "No one is to come with you!"

John Stott recommends one hour of solitude a day, one morning a week, one day a month and one week a year. And if you just cannot manage that (and he is, after all, both a bachelor and a pastor!), then plan what you can. Without discipline and stretching, we will never grow into Christ's likeness.

And husbands! If you do not already share the domestic load, insist on taking over some responsibilities to free your wives for time alone. They too need to grow!

The late Dr. Oswald Sanders, makes a valuable observation in *A Spiritual Clinic*. Under "The Strategic Use of Time," he notes that each person has 168 hours a week. Most spend 56 sleeping, 56 working and 21 on meals and devotions. While all have duties others do not have, these three most common basic needs take up 133 of the 168 hours. We are left with 35 hours, or 5 hours a day. From observation, Sanders concluded that the difference between one person and another was largely the difference in the way they spent those five hours a day. How do I measure up?

But how do I learn to spend time in solitude? I'm not sure how my previous suggestions on quietness will be received by a generation that seems to find noise in no way distracting. Some find it actually desirable, even essential, rather than face silence.

On asking one young pastor how he was able to prepare his sermon with the lyrics of a song resonating from his desk radio, he conceded he had to have noise. "But don't the words distract you from your need to think?" I asked.

"No way!" he said. "I don't even hear them!"

I am at a loss to explain how in two generations we have moved from craving silence to wanting noise. Has the hullabaloo itself created the ability? Perhaps in the same way cars find a detour around an accident or bacteria find a way to bypass the reproductive stage attacked by an antibiotic, this generation has become virtually immune to the exponential increase in noise.

Consequently, for some these days, silence is deafening!

On Mount Horeb Elijah heard the still small voice of God. But that "gentle whisper" was not heard in the noise of the wind, the earthquake or the fire. It was in the stillness that followed! (1 Kings 19:9-13). I still believe it is in silence that His voice is best heard.

Thinking It Through

Are you afraid of solitude? Do you feel uneasy when it's all quiet? Does whatever you do to compensate for that help or hinder you from hearing God's voice? Is there need to further adjust your response to silence?

Planting It Deep

"Whom have I in heaven but you?
And earth has nothing I desire besides you. . . .
But God is the strength of my heart
and my portion forever." (Psalm 73:25-26)

Praying It In

O Lord,
You who
set the solitary
in families
and dwell amidst
a million angels,
let me see You also
as the man Jesus,
forty days
alone
in the desert
and night after night
alone
on the mountain.
Show me the need
for both solitude and communion.
Teach me how
to hear Your voice
in the quiet,
so I'll recognize it
in the marketplace.
Amen.

GOD SCHEDULES THE ENCOUNTER

31

⌘

STEP 6: "Then the LORD came down." (Exodus 34:5)

Moses had met God's conditions. The encounter was imminent. "You will seek me and find me when you seek me with all your heart" (Jeremiah 29:13).

I am not always conscious of His presence. Some mornings my prayers seem to bounce off the ceiling. I pursue Him from a sense of duty. But my lack of detecting Him is surely due to my own changeableness, not God's. I would be concerned if weeks passed without my consciously encountering God. Could there be some lingering sin? Is there a failure to obey?

Sometimes without consciously seeking God, I encounter Him suddenly and with great surprise. Such encounters, when God invades my mediocrity, are not easily forgotten. One stands out clearly in my mind, although thirty years have passed.

I was standing on the bulldozed ruins of the "Sermons from Science" pavilion built for Expo '67 in Montreal. Alone and with no distraction, I found myself reliving its years of planning, building and actual operation under my direction. In two locations, this one the primary, 2.5 million people had witnessed the wonder and majesty of God's creation. One hundred sixty thousand had spent time in serious conversation with a counselor.

Guided by the telltale wall marks on the concrete floor, I made my way to the main auditorium. I had often stood against the rear wall, behind 300 seats, emptied and filled again every forty minutes. From here I could observe people and program, even the need to adjust the focus on the 16mm film. I called it my "focus-point."

Now, with no wall to lean back against and no screen to view, I gazed in that same direction. In my imagination I visualized the familiar sequences of a dozen films. I watched a "live demonstration" with Moody Institute of Science's George Speake standing on a coil and sending 1 million volts through his body. I could almost see the lightning from his fingers and the 2x4 bursting into flame in his hands.

Daydreaming over, my eyes fell once more on the ruins, now demolished in preparation for the 1976 Olympic Games. As I looked sentimentally towards the horizon, I saw what had not been visible while screen and walls blocked the view. Five miles away, across the St. Lawrence River, directly in line with the screen and on top of Mount Royal, was a 100-foot cross. Illuminated at night, and visible for miles around, it had replaced a wooden cross erected in 1643 by Chomedey de Maisonneuve in thanksgiving to God for saving the "colony" from flood.

I praised God as I thought of the 10,000 audiences—with untold numbers of changed lives—who had unknowingly gazed toward that cross.

At this point, it seemed that God came down into those ruins and stood with me. In my exhilaration, John Bowring's hymn came to my mind. Visiting the ruins of a church building while governor of Hong Kong generations ago, he had noticed the only wall still standing was topped by the cross.

Overcome with a sense of the permanence of the eternal, he penned those immortal words:

> In the Cross of Christ I glory
> Towering o'er the wrecks of time.[1]

Standing in the ruins, my head bowed, I thanked God for the privilege of having had a small part in extending His kingdom. My memories of the thousands confronted with the claims of Christ would fade with time, and the waters of the Olympic rowing basin would cover—maybe for centuries—the evidence of a pavilion; nevertheless I thanked Him that His cross, His kingdom and the eternal life now possessed by thousands would never wane.

Many times since, the Christ of Expo '67 has stepped out of the pages of the Bible to become a living reality. And while my emotions may have been less tugged, each experience took me a step further in cultivating a Christian lifestyle.

Thinking It Through

> He entered not by the eyes, for His presence was not marked by colour; nor by the ears, for there was no sound; nor by the breath, for He mingled not with the air; nor by the touch, for He was impalpable. You ask then, how I knew He was present. Because He was a quickening power. As soon as He entered, He awoke my slumbering soul; He moved and pierced my heart, which before was strange, stony, hard and sick, so that my soul could bless the Lord, and all that is within me praised His holy name.[2]

Planting It Deep

"All night long on my bed
I looked for the one my heart loves;
I looked for him but did not find him. . . .
I will search for the one my heart loves. . . .
I found the one my heart loves.
I held him and would not let him go."
(Song of Songs 3:1-2, 4)

Praying It In

O Lord,
thank You
for those special moments
when I have felt You close.
I long for
an even closer intimacy
that You may sow
Your seeds of love
into my life.
"Jesus, Lover of my soul,
let me to Your bosom fly."
Amen.

GOD TRIGGERS THE RESPONSE

32

STEP 7: "Moses bowed . . . and worshiped." (Exodus 34:8)

We can only guess the nature of Moses' encounter with God. But there's no doubt that what triggered Moses' worship was the character of God.

This was not the usual kind of theophany (God appearing as a man). Yet in some glorious way Moses saw God. Denied the privilege of seeing God's face, he did receive a fuller than previous, though still partial, manifestation.

In proclaiming His Name, the Lord shows Moses what He is like—compassionate, gracious, longsuffering, loving and faithful, qualities He wants us also to show others. It was this mind-boggling revelation of God's character that caused Moses to bow in worship.

We would do well to safeguard our worship against the need to be kindled by lower, less worthy motivation. While external stimuli often help direct us toward God, true worship does not depend primarily on such to get it going.

I mentioned earlier that I am in an isolated boat-house in a deserted cove on Canada's western shores. The breaking of the waves against the rocks, the frequent call of the Canada goose, the occasional sighting of a curious sea otter or a bald eagle perched atop the tallest tree all help me to be filled with wonder. It was this scene of beauty and solitude, unspoiled by human intrusion and framed with the awe-inspiring backdrop of glacial peaks, which drew me here.

But my worship may well be both felt and expressed just as effectively without such stimulating motivation. Indeed, there are times when the sheer beauty can compete to the point of distraction.

The same applies to good music (so appealing to my Welsh blood, especially in the minor key). Were I alone on a desert island, after my Bible, I would long for music. Yet even quiet music, without the distraction of lyrics or crashing crescendos, can be a barrier to worship. It takes just a few chords of Tomasso Albinoni's beautiful *Adagio* to leave its impact on me. But it usually grips a different part of my mind and emotions than I need for meditation and worship. It then becomes a distraction, subjectively enjoyable but counterproductive to my purpose.

When enjoying a praise time in church, I sometimes ask, "What is it about this that causes me to emote?" Is it the rhythm impacting my body? Is it the harmony appealing to my mind? Or is it the melody entrancing my spirit?

God—who made me spirit, mind and body—wants me to respond with all my being. (Read Psalm 63:1 again.) So while refusing morbid self-dissection, I nevertheless find it valuable to try and pinpoint what it is that mainly stimulates me to worship what I hope is God.

Moses' worship is triggered by nothing less than the truth about God's character (verses 6-7). When this grips my mind, it becomes the deepest of all incentives, drawing out my spirit in wondrous praise.

Only then can melody, harmony and rhythm help me to express authentically what has impacted my mind. Anything less can deteriorate into a worship of worship. Such subjective enjoyment may send a thrill up my spine, but has little to do with worshiping God.

Here then is the watershed test. When the instruments have stopped, the Bible opened and the character of God expounded, does my worship deepen or diminish? If the latter, I would do well to plan periods of absolute quietness, until my mind, singly focused on God Himself, learns to respond in unaided worship.

Once that lesson is learned I will be in less danger of making too much of outward aids. Only then can I more safely use every faculty, as well as the rhythm and harmony of beautiful melodies, to more richly enjoy my worship.

It is when "my heart finds rest in God alone" (Psalm 62:1) that my body, and "all that is within me" can "praise His holy name." Such motivation will then produce right living after the music has stopped.

Thinking It Through

While we must remember that "God is spirit, and his worshipers must worship in spirit and in truth" (John 4:24), we must beware of bypassing our minds, which God continually renews with His truth. That truth then penetrates the spirit, to be set on fire by God's Spirit. Contemplation then grows out of meditation, reaching a climax in praise and adoration.

Planting It Deep

"No one knows the thoughts of God except the Spirit of God. We have not received the spirit of the world, but the Spirit who is from God, that we may understand what God has freely given us. This is what we speak, not in words taught us by human wisdom but in words taught by the Spirit, expressing spiritual truths in spiritual words. . . . We have the mind of Christ." (1 Corinthians 2:11-13, 16)

Praying It In

O Lord,
I am often
so selfish
in my worship.
It is supposed to be
an act of unselfish giving,
something for You, not me!
Help me to see
that what benefits me
is only the by-product.
Fill my mind and my heart
with an understanding
of Your character,
that I may sincerely worship
YOU,
both in spirit and in truth.
Amen.

THE SECRET OF A RADIANT LIFE

33

THE SEQUEL: "His face was radiant." (Exodus 34:29)

They could see it on his face! Moses had been with God. His reflecting God's glory gave him an attentive audience for God's words. Yet he "was not aware his face was radiant." Those who shine the brightest are least aware of their influence. They are more aware of God's holiness and their own sinfulness.

"Because he had spoken with the LORD," Moses reflected Him. We too will reflect His character as we commune unhurriedly with Him. Others may speak with eloquence, but only those who gaze on God can reflect His beauty to a needy world.

Did Nathaniel Hawthorne have this biblical incident in mind when he wrote, "The Great Stone Face"?

It is the story of a boy, Ernest, who lived in the shadow of a mountain, on which he could see an amazing natural phenomenon, the noble features of what was known by the villagers as "The Great Stone Face." A legend foretold that one day a child born in the village would become the noblest person of his time; his face in manhood would bear an exact resemblance to the Great Stone Face.

Every spare moment, Ernest would turn his face upwards and gaze at those desirable features. If only the kindly-looking figure would talk, he was sure his voice would be so pleasant, and he would love him dearly.

On three occasions as Ernest grew up, rumors spread that the long-awaited figure was about to appear. But the rich merchant, the illustrious soldier and the statesman with eloquent tongue were all disappointments.

As Ernest grew into old age, he kept gazing at the Great Stone Face. His admiration and longing to meet the one who would resemble it also grew.

Still more years passed. Now with white hair and wrinkled forehead, Ernest became possessed with a fame unsought and undesired; a fame others may long to have. Wise men came from far and wide to seek his counsel, not gained from books, but from, they were persuaded, his having conversed with angels. He received them with that gentle serenity which grew even more mellow as he aged.

One day, a man of great literary genius returned to the village. All believed that surely now the noble figure had arrived. Even Ernest, who had fondly read this poet's work, held high hopes this was the one.

It was not long before the poet confided his life had not corresponded with the high ideals of his thought and poetry. "I have had grand dreams," he told Ernest, "but they remain dreams because I have chosen to live among poor and mean realities. I lack faith in the beauty and goodness which my own words have made more evident in nature and in human life." He spoke sadly, his eyes dimmed with tears. So, likewise, were Ernest's.

At sunset it was Ernest's custom to speak in the open air to the local residents. That day, he and the poet walked there arm in arm. As Ernest addressed them, the villagers sensed great power in his words, because they sincerely echoed his lifestyle.

The poet could not help but notice the Great Stone Face high up behind Ernest. The setting sun and the hoary mists gave it the appearance of the white hairs around Ernest's brow. That beneficent Face seemed to embrace the world.

"At that moment," says Nathaniel Hawthorne, finishing his story, "the face of Ernest assumed a grandeur of expression, so imbued with benevolence, that the poet, by an irresistible impulse, threw his arms aloft and shouted, 'Behold! Behold! Ernest is himself the likeness of the Great Stone Face.' "

The people agreed. The legend was fulfilled. But Ernest took the poet's arm and walked slowly home, still hoping some wiser and better man than himself would shortly appear.[1]

Had Hawthorne read about Moses? Had not Ernest's gazing had a parallel effect? What fills our gaze leaves its unmistakable impression upon us.

Thinking It Through

Radiance of being and impact of presence come less from the words we speak than from the lives we live. Made in God's image, He wants us to reflect Him. Do we gaze at God as often as Ernest in our story looked at the Great Stone Face? If not, how could we start doing that today?

Planting It Deep

"I keep asking that the God of our Lord Jesus Christ, the glorious Father, may give you the Spirit of wisdom and revelation, so that you may know him better. I pray also that the eyes of your heart may be enlightened in order that you may know the hope to which he has called you, the riches of his glorious inheritance in the saints, and his incomparably great power for us who believe." (Ephesians 1:17-19)

Praying It In

O Lord,
I long to be
single-minded!
I want my thoughts
to be centered on You!
Without neglecting
my own part in
bringing this about,
I now submit my mind
to Your Spirit.
Lord, open my eyes
that I may see!
Amen.

A Prayer

O Lord,
how privileged I am
to be Your child,
one of Your family.

I never cease to be amazed
that You, the great Creator,
became my Savior.

And as if that were not enough,
You now bring me
into Your banqueting house
and Your banner over me
is love.

I so enjoy those times there, Lord,
in Your presence,
feasting on Your Word.
But I revel in the added blessing
of going even further
and seeing You Yourself.

Those times with You
on the mountaintop
are so special
They have become for me
the most precious part
of my relationship.

And I really just wanted to say
a genuine thank You;

but then realized
that words can be so empty.
So instead I want to
simply make myself available
to be a small reflection of You.

So Lord, as I
with pure motive
and disciplined life
climb Your mountain
to meet You each morning,
would You show me Your glory?
Then let my life so reflect it
that people will say
"He has been with Jesus—
we can see it in his life!"

Amen.

PART FOUR

Contemplating

2 Corinthians 3:12-18

[12]*Therefore, since we have such a hope, we are very bold.* [13]*We are not like Moses, who would put a veil over his face to keep the Israelites from gazing at it while the radiance was fading away.* [14]*But their minds were made dull, for to this day the same veil remains when the old covenant is read. It has not been removed, because only in Christ is it taken away.* [15]*Even to this day when Moses is read, a veil covers their hearts.* [16]*But whenever anyone turns to the Lord, the veil is taken away.* [17]*Now the Lord is the Spirit, and where the Spirit of the Lord is, there is freedom.* [18]*And we, who with unveiled faces all reflect the Lord's glory, are being transformed into his likeness with ever-increasing glory, which comes from the Lord, who is the Spirit.*

FROM MEDITATION TO CONTEMPLATION

34

"But we all, with unveiled face beholding as in a mirror
the glory of the Lord, are being transformed into the same image
from glory to glory, just as from the Lord, the Spirit."
(2 Corinthians 3:18, NASB)

Contemplation is not the exclusive occupation of hermits or desert fathers. It is essential for a godly lifestyle and should accompany meditation.

While Christian meditation loves to lose itself in the minutiae of the Word, Christian contemplation, standing on the shoulders of meditation, sees into the very throne room of God Himself until it becomes "lost in wonder, love and praise."

These two vital elements of our communion with God work best together. On its own, without the right goal, meditation on Scripture can deteriorate into an exercise in mental gymnastics. Then again, subjective mystical contemplation, unless anchored to the Rock of the Word, runs the risk of being swept away by strange currents into uncharted seas.

Perhaps our use of the term "Bible study" subconsciously conjures up the thought of a textbook and an examination. Good though such knowledge is, it misses the mark unless it pursues the adoration of God Himself. Mary Lathbury captured the thought well in her much-sung hymn, "Break Thou the Bread of Life."

> Beyond the sacred page
> I seek Thee, Lord;
> My spirit pants for Thee,
> O living Word.[1]

In our previous segments we have been examining the words of Scripture. How wonderful to know they are God-breathed, inspired by the Holy Spirit. Being careful to build on that foundation of meditation, we shall now prepare ourselves to be carried in our spirits—and by that same Holy Spirit—into the place where we can worship and adore God Himself.

Contemplation is gazing at and worshiping with adoration the One who is described in the Scriptures we have been studying. As with Moses in the last several pages, it is this gazing at God's glory which brings about the change that both pleases God and impacts the world.

On my travels, I carry with me what I call my "worship wallet." It contains some specially loved verses of hymns which mean a lot to me. They help focus my mind on the Lord Jesus. Here is one which I frequently use. Try pondering it as preparation for our next meditation.

> Jesus, wondrous Saviour! Christ of kings
>   the King!
> Angels fall before Thee, prostrate, worshiping;
> Fairest they confess Thee, in the heav'n above,
> We would sing Thee fairest, here in hymns of
>   love.
>
> All earth's flowing pleasures were a wintry sea;
> Heav'n itself without Thee, dark as night would be.
> Lamb of God! Thy glory is the light above,
> Lamb of God! Thy glory is Thy deathless love.

Life is death if severed from Thy throbbing heart,
Death, to life abundant, at Thy touch would start.
Worlds and men and angels all consist in Thee;
Yet Thou camest to us, in humility.

Jesus! All perfections rise and end in Thee;
Brightness of God's glory, Thou eternally!
Favoured beyond measure, they Thy face
    who see;
May we, gracious Saviour, share this ecstasy.[2]

Close your eyes and imagine yourself in the very throne room of God, prostrate, worshiping. Let the thoughts of this hymn fully occupy your mind. Tell the Lord Jesus how much you love and adore Him.

Like other disciplines, this will take some getting used to. Although some days will not be as good as others, you can be sure that over the months, if you keep at it, you will begin to find it your greatest joy.

Thinking It Through

We are in danger of substituting the understanding of concepts for the experiencing of the reality—so said Tozer, in different words at different times. Are you satisfied with having merely read this segment, or would you like to pursue it further? What is it you now need so as to be able to commune in your spirit with God?

Planting It Deep

"And I pray that you, being rooted and established in love, may have power, together with all the saints, to grasp how wide and long and high and deep is the love of Christ, and to know this love that surpasses knowledge—that you may be filled to the measure of all the fullness of God." (Ephesians 3:17-19)

Praying It In

O Lord,
I find it so hard
to "set the stage"
to properly contemplate You
without distraction.
But I realize
I must keep on trying.
Would You give me
that grace of perseverance,
so I will persist
even when I feel like giving up?
Amen.

WHY WE FIND IT
HARD TO CONTEMPLATE

35

*"But we all, with unveiled face beholding as in a mirror
the glory of the Lord, are being transformed into the same image
from glory to glory, just as from the Lord, the Spirit."
(2 Corinthians 3:18, NASB)*

D r. Tozer or one of his contemporaries—memory fails me which—suggested to me forty years ago four reasons why we were gradually losing the art of Christian contemplation. As far as I recall, here, in my own words and headings, is the gist of what I learned.

1. The Concrete Jungle

Many of us have moved from quiet country lanes to busy city streets. Concrete jungles and crowded subways are a far cry from rolling meadows and roaming herds. Distractions have increased a hundredfold. Everyone wants to get his message across, bombarding us with information we never wanted. They keep on coming from all directions—by telephone, by radio, by computer, by billboard. Words! Words! Words! At night they're in lights—moving, blinking! It all leaves us little opportunity to think about God.

2. The "I Want It Now" Society

Toffler's *Future Shock* vividly portrayed our insatiable appetite for time-saving devices. With disposable dishes, instant cameras, microwave ovens and ATMs, we have succeeded in producing a computerized generation that wants everything without waiting. And even when the Internet provides it, we don't even like having to wait to boot up the computer.

This malaise has infected the Church. Instant holiness is now part of the expectation of Sunday "worshipers" who roll out of bed at 10:40 and slide into the pew at one minute past 11. Conditioned by TV, we expect we can "change channels" and instantly be in tune with our Maker. But it takes time to be holy!

3. The Belittling of Monarchs

At twelve years old, I was part of a Welsh schoolboys' choir. We were to perform Handel's *Messiah* on three successive Saturdays at Swansea's Brangwyn Hall. One Saturday, the large concert hall had been cleared. On three solitary chairs just thirty feet from me sat King George VI, his queen, and Princess (now Queen) Elizabeth. I was awestruck!

Following tradition, the royal party stood for the Hallelujah Chorus. The king was a true believer. The intensity of his upward look with closed eyes (not the norm for reserved British monarchs!), left a profound impression upon me. He was my king; I stood in awe of him. Yet at this moment he was standing to pay homage to the King of kings.

That scene has never faded from my memory. Since that day I think about God as the King my king worshiped! Earthly monarchs helped us conceptualize God. But we now stand less in awe than we did. When a royal figure is morally or politically deplumed, our concept of majesty shrinks; and with it, our ability to fall prostrate in worship before God.

To experience the wonder, splendor and majesty of God, as did Isaiah, Ezekiel or John, is something strangely lacking in Western Christianity. And when this begins to evaporate, there seems little point in contemplation.

4. The Busy, Buzzing Church

We used to go to church to see God. But activity has largely replaced meditation; noise has supplanted quietness; entertainment has superseded ministry; and programs have almost taken over from the preaching of the Bible.

Seldom do we encourage quietness to think at the start or the close of a service. We rush into public prayer with pocketed hands, little reverence and no time for examination. The invocation, which used to lift the worshiper into the presence of God, is now rarely more than a quick sentence, with the organ chomping at the bit. The pastoral prayer, once as prominent as the sermon, scarcely lasts more than two minutes to give time for things more appealing. The church, once the model for meditation, now hardly seems to practice it at all.

Our lives are likely to become increasingly rushed and crowded. As we speed up our frantic search for shortcuts, filling gaps with action-packed projects, we shall be less and less able to discover the majesty of God. But there is an answer!

Thinking It Through

Having read these four probable reasons for being less able to contemplate, we now need to ponder them awhile. We must determine which ones have adversely affected our ability to commune with God. This will give us more incentive to find the answer.

Planting It Deep

"This is what the Sovereign LORD, the Holy One of Is-rael, says:

*'In repentance and rest is your salvation,
   in quietness and trust is your strength. . . .' "*
      (Isaiah 30:15)

Praying It In

O Lord,
I'm back again,
with the same old excuse,
B-U-S-Y-N-E-S-S !
What's the point
of my trying
to minimize distractions
when I've not even the time
to contemplate You?
Why do I keep on asking You
to adjust my schedule?
Isn't it time
I took
the responsibility myself?
As I try,
will You pour into me
courage,
wisdom,
and discipline?
Thank You, Lord.
Amen.

THE ANSWER TO OUR FRUSTRATION

36

*"But we all, with unveiled face beholding as in a mirror
the glory of the Lord, are being transformed into the same image
from glory to glory, just as from the Lord, the Spirit."
(2 Corinthians 3:18, NASB)*

I never cease to wonder at the wisdom which packs the pages of the Bible. It seems that there is guidance—guaranteed to work—for every essential area of life. And the longing to become like Jesus Christ is no exception.

Take that inability to contemplate, which we saw in our last segment. There is a way out of it! But before we look into it, let me suggest four little thoughts to tuck away in your mind for frequent pondering. They will help you grow until you have properly mastered the wonderful habit we shall see in our verse:

1. Cultivate the ability to switch off surrounding distractions. In other words, practice inward withdrawal. Attitudinal solitude requires no special location. "There is a place of quiet rest, near to the heart of God." I can find it in a crowded airport. Keep trying. If it does not come, then for today try sitting alone in your car, windows closed. And if it still eludes you, try again tomorrow.

2. *Take the long route whenever you can.* Shortcuts are not always productive. They often rob us of time to think or relax. The time we save is not usually spent on important things, like thinking about God, but on "fire fighting" other equally time-consuming problems of the day.

Wherever possible we need to think more deeply and learn to abide. But that takes time. Meanwhile try leaving the car half a mile down the road so you can walk and get time to think. Take the stairway instead of the elevator (unless your doctor forbids). Even six floors won't kill most of us!

3. *Carry a New Testament and Psalms in your pocket or purse.* Use the minutes while you are waiting for something (like the coffee brewing, the bus arriving, or your turn at the bank teller), to read those scriptures which emphasize God's majesty, greatness and justice. Hear the kingly words of Jesus. Focus on the love of God displayed on the cross.

4. *Balance each activity with a time of quietness.* This need not be long to start. Just get it going. Take enough time to fix your eyes on Jesus and determine His purpose in the activity you've just finished or are about to start.

> Turn your eyes upon Jesus,
>   Look full in His wonderful face,
> And the things of earth will grow strangely dim
>   In the light of His glory and grace.[1]

Thankfully, our gracious and understanding God meets us where we are, not where He thinks we ought to be. Our primary verse for counteracting the pull of the whirling world is Second Corinthians 3:18: "But we all, with unveiled face beholding as in a mirror the glory of the Lord, are being transformed into the same image from glory to glory, just as from the Lord, the Spirit" (NASB). Those who are truly thirsting after God will find themselves drawn more and more deeply into this rich teaching about the Christ-filled life.

The more we contemplate God, the more we will become like Him. It is an unchanging, guaranteed recipe for becoming a transformed person. This verse, indeed the whole second half of this Bible chapter, is the New Testament commentary on the Exodus 34 passage we saw earlier in this book. But here we are given even more insight into cultivating that thirst after God.

We shall break the verse into its two parts: First my part, then God's. *My part is contemplation* (beholding the glory of the Lord). *God's part is transformation* (changing me into Christ's likeness).

Thinking It Through

Do you sometimes say, "I could never do that! It's not my thing! Not my gift, not my personality!" Yet I've been surprised when I try something I thought just wasn't me: I usually succeed. Could it be that practicing the ideas in this segment will have more to do with your attitude than your aptitude?

Planting It Deep

"I have chosen you. . . .
    I am with you;
    do not be dismayed, for I am your God.
I will strengthen you and help you;
    I will uphold you with my righteous right hand."
        (Isaiah 41:9-10)

Praying It In

O Lord,
You know
I often have big ideas—
so big
I keep putting them off!
And even those I start well,
I rarely finish.
I don't want to be
like an Alka-Seltzer—
all fizz, and then nothing!
Give me grace
to start small
rather than not at all!
Amen.

CLEAR THE OBSTACLES

37

*"But we all, with unveiled face beholding as in a mirror
the glory of the Lord, are being transformed into the same image
from glory to glory, just as from the Lord, the Spirit."*
(2 Corinthians 3:18, NASB)

I cannot overemphasize the need to prepare our hearts if we long to see anything of the glory of the Lord. Do you recall that Moses had to "present" himself before the Lord? That took some thoughtful preparation!

The first of the three steps to become like the Lord Jesus is coming "with unveiled face." I have chosen to use the New American Standard Bible for this verse. Don't be distracted if your Bible version uses "reflecting" or "contemplating" instead of "beholding." Half translate one way and half the other. The original word likely includes both thoughts. Indeed, reflecting the Light is not possible without beholding it. But we shall talk about this later.

I've called this first one "Clear the Obstacles." Make sure there is nothing between you and God. If we are going to spend time contemplating the glory of the Lord, we must be sure there is no barrier (here called a "veil") which will obstruct God's rays from having their full effect on us.

"With unveiled face" primarily refers back to verses 14-16, and Exodus 34:33-35, where the veil, which made our minds dull and unable to see the truth, is removed. This happens when we "turn to the Lord" or become a Christian. We often say that someone has "seen the Light," suggesting the veil has gone.

So if we are thirsting for God and have never responded to His overtures by turning to Him, the obvious priority for us right now is to do that. Coming in repentance and faith, we must turn from our selfish ways to follow Christ. The veil in its primary sense will then be removed.

In a lesser, secondary sense, I think of a veil as anything which comes between even a Christian and God. For instance, unconfessed sin in our lives means that God cannot look upon us until we confess and ask forgiveness. Otherwise there is a wall between me and God. Psalm 66:18 says, "If I regard iniquity in my heart, the Lord will not hear me" (KJV). The veil which blocked my understanding has gone, but another veil, one which prevents my communing with my Heavenly Father, has taken its place.

Maybe you are already a Christian but long for God to be with you in a more meaningful way. You thirst after God, yet He still seems to elude you, so you find no satisfaction. Let me suggest that as you read, you allow the Holy Spirit to put His finger on the painful areas of unconfessed sin. I find that kneeling at my bed with my hands covering my face makes it easier for me to detect those things on my conscience. But you know what works best for you.

There is no need to morbidly submit yourself to an unhealthy personal inquisition in which you dig up muck from your soul's ocean bed, determined to find something unworthy lurking in the darkness of the deep. No! Deal with whatever God reveals to you. If you are faithful in this, He will swing the searchlight of His Word onto other areas in His good time. Live up to the light God gives you and you'll be sure to receive more.

One evening I was replacing two burned-out screw-in fuses underneath the back of our kitchen stove. I had purchased six new ones and picked up one from the bag to screw in. I flipped the switch on, but nothing happened. *It must be a dud,* I thought. I put it aside and tried the second. Same result. Then a third! Annoyed at the store manager, I thought, *Could it be that they're all duds?* But one more look at the fuses showed that it was I who was the dud! The price label was wrapped with scotch tape right around the thread of the fuse! The channel for the communication of power was obstructed. I removed the obstruction and all was well.

It's the same with confession of sin. Exposing sin for what it is removes the veil in that secondary sense. It is the spiritual equivalent of removing a sun umbrella so as to expose your sun-starved body to the light and warmth of the summer sun. You will notice the change very quickly.

Thinking It Through

Have you thanked God that when He moved you to trust Him for salvation, He undid Satan's hold over your blinded eyes? But do you realize that unconfessed sin can still act as a plastic insulator over your battery connection? The light won't go on! The obstacle can be removed only by confession. Will you do it?

Planting It Deep

"The god of this age has blinded the minds of unbelievers, so that they cannot see the light of the gospel of the glory of Christ, who is the image of God." (2 Corinthians 4:4)

Praying It In

O Lord,
I'm always looking
for someone else to blame.
Saying
"The devil made me do it"
gets me off the hook!
But I know the problem
is sin!
My sin!
The one
I don't want to give up!
I need to see
You in all Your holiness, Lord.
Then perhaps I will grasp
the utter sinfulness
of my sin.
Do soften my heart
as I read these chapters.
Amen.

FACE THE RIGHT DIRECTION

38

*"But we all, with unveiled face beholding as in a mirror
the glory of the Lord, are being transformed into the same image
from glory to glory, just as from the Lord, the Spirit."*
(2 Corinthians 3:18, NASB)

Having put things right, we must now secondly, face the glory we want to reflect. Being finite, we cannot face the direct blaze of God's glory. We'll have to settle for being one stage removed from direct vision, like light refracted through a prism, or the sun reflected off the ocean.

We must remember that this "reflected glory" is not the only reason why the concept of a mirror is used in our verse—but more of that later. Ponder with me, first, four places where God's glory is reflected:

1. God's glory is reflected in the heavens. "The heavens declare the glory of God" (Psalm 19:1). Looking up at night we see the wonders of God's creation. We consider God's omnipotence in calling into being one galaxy after another. We ask with the psalmist, "What is man that You are mindful of him . . . ?" (8:4).

2. God's glory is reflected in the pages of history. Measuring time by centuries, we can see God's timetable. On the chessboard of history, people on the one side and events on the other seem to move almost inexorably toward the final checkmate.

God's omniscience was behind it; His providence brought it about.

3. God's glory is reflected in the faces of His people. Apart from physiological differences, we can often (I wish I could say always) spot the difference between genuine Christians and others. It is something called "physiognomy," a word which aptly describes "the capacity of the face to reveal what is in the soul."

It's not something put on or just a bubble bath of perpetual emotion. It bursts out from the confinement of the inner life and is expressed not only in the face, but in mind, emotions and will, indeed, the whole life. It is the beauty of Jesus, the telltale evidence of a living faith, the reflected glory of God! And the possessors are rarely conscious they possess it.

4. God's glory is reflected in His Word, the Bible. This special reflection mirrors God's attributes in perfect balance. It tells me how to become more like Jesus. Inspired by God, it was penned by men who were "carried along" by the Holy Spirit (2 Peter 1:21). It even likens itself to a mirror (James 1:23-25) in which we see both God and ourselves. As I read it, I feel the Writer knows me through and through; my longings and my evil tendencies. Just as I look into a mirror to see my face, so I look into the mirror of the Word to see the condition of my soul.

I once heard the late Stan Ford, a South of England boxing champion, tell of visiting New York in the '50s. He was attracted to a window with several spotlights all focused on one beautiful necktie. Irresistibly drawn, he found himself in a room walled by mirrors. An immaculately dressed man appeared. "Yes sir, the necktie?" He brought it from a back room. Stan put on the pièce de résistance and checked himself in the mirror. It looked great. That is, until he noticed his impeccably dressed friend standing beside him. Only then did he notice the flaws in his shirt collar.

Sensing his uneasiness, the clerk suggested, "Sir, may I show you a shirt?" He returned with a dress shirt and repeated the procedure. Once more, delight was followed by concern as he further compared himself with the dapper image beside him. Of course, he finished up buying the lot—tie, shirt and suit! The clever plan had worked!

Aren't we the same? We fail to see how shabby we are until we compare ourselves with flawlessness. The Bible mirror gives us such a comparison. We see ourselves alongside the perfect image of Christ. We feel like skulking away in disgrace.

There is a fifth place I can see God's glory. It is the most important of all, but because this is *un*-reflected glory, we look by faith rather than by sight. It is the very Person of Jesus Himself. While we meditate on the mirror of the Bible by sight, it requires faith to see beyond the words and gaze at the Person of the Risen Christ. In order to prepare for such contemplative ecstasy, you should, after the prayer below, read Rabbit Trail #2.

Thinking It Through

Ponder the fact that you cannot look directly at God's great glory. It would blind you, blow your mind, and—apart from Jesus—end your life. You would be dumbstruck at His brightness and holiness. Thank God for His grace in letting you peer at Him dimly, through a mirror. One day it will be face-to-face!

Planting It Deep

"For God, who said, 'Let light shine out of darkness,' made his light shine in our hearts to give us the light of the knowledge of the glory of God in the face of Christ." (2 Corinthians 4:6)

Praying It In

O Lord,
I am so thankful
that although
my faith is small,
it's in the right place—
in You!
Lord, increase my faith,
that by it
I may see
Him who is invisible,
and that "by faith"
I shall also be able
to contemplate Your glory
in the face of Jesus Christ!
Amen.

GAZE UPON GOD

39

*"But we all, with unveiled face beholding as in a mirror
the glory of the Lord, are being transformed into the same image
from glory to glory, just as from the Lord, the Spirit."*
(2 Corinthians 3:18, NASB)

We now come to the last of our three steps in contemplating God.

Having watched two teenage daughters grow into womanhood, I can tell the difference between the way they look at a watch and the way they look into a mirror. Recognizing this difference is important if we are going to understand how to cultivate the art of contemplating God.

It takes five English words—"beholding as in a mirror"—to translate the central word of our verse from the New Testament language. It could be translated "mirroring," but because mirroring is too ambiguous, the translators chose either the beholding mode (RSV, NASB, KJV, Knox, etc.) or the reflecting mode (NIV, RV, NEB, Jerusalem, etc.). Several put the other word in the footnote as equally allowable.

We must understand the difficulty the translators have; it is like deciding whether "he breathed" means he breathed in or he breathed out. To breathe in means to receive something from outside; to breathe out means to give out (a changed form of) what was received. When we behold (or receive) the glory of the Lord we are then able to reflect (give out).

The translation "reflecting" was felt to fit best with the context, but several word specialists insisted that this form of the word means "beholding" (the NIV footnote is "or contemplating").

We shall therefore respect both views. For just as I can empty my lungs only if I have filled them, so I can reflect only what I behold. But the converse is also true: If I am not reflecting Christ in life and behavior, I am certainly not spending significant time beholding Him. One of God's laws of holiness is, "The more we contemplate God, the more we shall become like Him."

We saw something of the reflecting in our last segment in that the glory we behold is *reflected* glory. We shall also think more later about our becoming reflectors ourselves. But because beholding the glory of the Lord takes much time (and indeed a key reason for choosing this word may be so as to include the concept of "prolonged gazing"—as we do in a mirror), we shall for now focus on the "beholding" mode. We'll see what it means to "behold as in a mirror the glory of the Lord."

This is no quick glance. It is an extended gaze, as when a woman may redo a complicated hair arrangement after a long night's sleep. It takes time! (Indeed, we could do worse than use that as a guide to the minimum time spent privately gazing upon God.)

Also, a word to the wise about meditating, which is, after all, the best foundation for contemplating. As I behold God's glory, it is essential I use the Bible as my primary meditation for God to disclose Himself. It is in this special revelation—the Holy Scriptures—even more than in His general revelation in creation, that I will see God's glory clearly. God's Word is a reflection of God's heart. The more I read it, the more I will thirst after God.

We need not wonder then why this Bible is the safest foundation on which to build the habit of contemplating God. Meditation on the Word primarily occupies the mind. It sets up a defense mechanism to prevent the evil one from passing off his lies as truth. It is in the Bible that I see God's true character. Storing Scripture will therefore give me the capacity to filter out wrong thoughts about Him. It also makes me less vulnerable to being drawn into strange worship ideas or a false mysticism.

As I ponder the knowledge of the Holy (which happens also to be the title of a superb book by Tozer on the attributes of God), I will be like the wise man, building my house of contemplation upon the rock of Scripture. And should God reveal something to my spirit which my mind cannot yet grasp (as can happen to all of us), the saturation with the Word will keep me on the right track.

Thinking It Through

Years ago, children played with one toy for hours. I have noticed how rare this is today. We are all conditioned to move fast, not linger. Have you been sucked into the system? Do you get fidgety if left alone too long? I am amazed how quickly I get tired (or bored?) kneeling in the middle of the floor with my back upright. Try it! How long can you go? Have we lost something?

Planting It Deep

"Be still, and know that I am God." (Psalm 46:10)

Praying It In

O Lord,
How we have changed
since
the world was younger.
Stillness
no longer comes easily.
I keep on moving
so that I get no benefit
from what I was doing.
Teach me again
the art
of quietness and serenity;
show me
that the best things in life
take time!
Amen.

KEEP GAZING

40

*"But we all, with unveiled face beholding as in a mirror
the glory of the Lord, are being transformed into the same image
from glory to glory, just as from the Lord, the Spirit."
(2 Corinthians 3:18, NASB)*

We continue our move from studying words in meditation to beholding God in contemplation. This
takes place primarily in your spirit, as you pour out your love
and adoration to the Lord. The Holy Spirit will take the fuel
fed to your mind as you meditate on the Word, and set it on
fire in your spirit. I often reach a stage in my meditation where
a truth so grips me I just have to burst into praise.

Mark you, there are many mornings when I simply do not
have that experience. At those times I still close my eyes and
seek, by faith, to see God. But then it is not with the same
overwhelming desire. Yet, despite this, after I determine to do
what is right, my emotions catch up. Minutes later I find myself rejoicing that I moved—in spite of the lack of desire—into
the contemplating stage.

As the sense of God's presence becomes more real I start to
sing love songs to Him. The songs I sing are usually from two
sources: a hymnbook and the "worship wallet" I referred to earlier. This gives me a balance of richly worded theology and sub-

jectively appealing chorus songs. Mostly I find myself using the first thirty or so hymns from this hymnbook which hold rich memories for me. So many of them address God directly in the second person (Thou, Thine, You or Your). This easily enables me to close my eyes and turn the hymn into a prayer.

After filling my mind with such rich theology, I use my little worship wallet, containing the bits of paper on which I have scribbled thoughts about God, helpful prayers or love songs from the chorus tradition. So many of these help move my spirit in worship.

I have one sheet, its folds now splitting, on which I have jotted the first line of thirty or forty songs I know well, such as "Jesus, Jesus, Jesus, there's just something about that Name," or "Your Name is as ointment poured forth." That first line is all I need to get going. In addition, I have written one meaningful verse from each of a dozen hymns like, "Where is the blessedness I knew when first I saw the Lord?" or "Jesus, Thou joy of loving hearts" by my favorite hymnwriter, Bernard of Clairvaux.

Alone one morning, I was reading Revelation 4 and 5. I made an effort to roughly sketch John's description of the Throne of God, the sea, the Lamb, the sevenfold Spirit of God, the living creatures and elders, the angelic host and every creature in heaven and earth. It was beyond me, but my badly scribbled concentric circles still help me see the reality of what may otherwise pass me by.

In such intimate times I am often oblivious to the hands of the clock. Those hours are surely a foretaste of a timeless eternity worshiping the Lord. Most days, however, my watch beeper will go off, rudely pulling me back from being lost in worship and making me realize I am not privileged to live in a cloister but in a demanding world of deadlines.

Frankly, I have come to appreciate the balance of solitude and service.

I am usually glad I forced myself out of bed, because those precious times with the Lord set the tone for the whole day.

Having removed the veil, faced the glory and gazed upon God, our verse gives me confidence to believe I can now depend on God to do His part. That's next!

Thinking It Through

If your worship is "spiritual," it comes from your spirit—not just from your mind. Yet your mind, renewed in Christ, feeds your spirit. That fuel is then set on fire. Since you came to faith, the pilot flame burns continuously in your spirit. Test yourself often, to check how long it takes for the fuel to catch on fire. Is the pilot light really burning brightly?

Planting It Deep

"You, O LORD, keep my lamp burning;
my God turns my darkness into light."
(Psalm 18:28)

Praying It In

O Lord,
There was a time
when I knew
You'd set my heart on fire.
But the flame
has been burning low of late.
It is still alight,
but it takes so long
to set Your Word on fire
in my heart.
I want it
to burn brightly again, Lord.
As I ponder these truths,
will You show me
what I can do?
And then take over,
to do Yourself
what I cannot do.
Amen.

THE CHANGE WILL BE CERTAIN

41

*"But we all, with unveiled face beholding as in a mirror
the glory of the Lord, are being transformed into the same image
from glory to glory, just as from the Lord, the Spirit."
(2 Corinthians 3:18, NASB)*

There are few things left on earth which man is not able
to transform. One tap of a finger on a computer key-
board can in seconds bring such technological change in a
hundred countries that emperors and presidents of past generations would turn in their graves in utter astonishment.
Even Dolly, the first cloned sheep, soon produced normal off-
spring and disappeared into the scientific history books.

But there is one thing that continues to elude man: How to
bring about a radical moral change, transforming self-centered
rebels into loving, caring and productive members of society.
Only God the Holy Spirit can genuinely bring about such a
change. This is what Second Corinthians 3:18 is all about. We
saw the principle it teaches: The more we contemplate God, the
more we shall become like Him.

We have cleared the obstacles which prevented us seeing
God. We have learned the direction we must face to see Him.
And we have seen what it means to gaze unhurriedly and
undistractedly on His glory. We have met all the conditions of

this law of holiness. Now it is up to God to bring about the change.

Three things will happen in our lives, as seen in part two of verse 18. We will examine one in each of these three segments. They are

1. The change will be certain
2. The likeness will be unmistakable
3. The process will be gradual.

Yes, *the change will be certain!* For the transformation described in our verse is more than a promise, good though that is in itself. It is the inevitable consequence of gazing upon God. Our text says we "all" are being transformed. As sure as day follows night and spring follows winter, all who contemplate God will be transformed. It's the law. No exceptions!

How easy it is to think that we ourselves can bring about the change. But such is impossible, for our verse says it is "from the Lord, the Spirit." "We are being transformed" indicates that someone else, in this case the Holy Spirit, brings about the change when we meet the conditions.

"Look at the suntan I got myself in Hawaii," says a bronzed teenager. But all he did was put himself in the right position—on Waikiki Beach when the sun was shining. It was not he, but the sun, that gave him the tan.

"All right," he says, thinking I'm nit-picking, "I was so hot I jumped in the water and cooled myself off!"

"Wrong again," I say, "I agree you had to jump in the water, but it was the water that cooled you off!"

"Oh, come on," he says, "everyone says it that way!" And that is exactly our problem. For if we say it wrongly enough times, we shall begin to think wrongly. In actuality all we can do is to set the stage and meet the conditions. God alone can do the work of bringing about the change!

I say, "Look at the photos I took." But did I really take them? All I did was to press a button which opened a window and let the light strike the film inside my camera. It was the light, not I, that put the image on the film. To some, it may seem semantic trivia. But it is anything but trivial if it will teach me how I am to grow in godliness.

In contemplating God, I merely set the stage. The Holy Spirit does the transforming. To put my quiet time into photographic language, I expose the film of my life to the Light of the world. It is that Light, by His Spirit that imprints the image on my character.

And every time I behold God's glory, the change will be certain!

Thinking It Through

We live in an entrepreneurial age. We can change anything. We have problems with being stumped. It takes humility to accept defeat, or see someone else succeed where you failed. Are you transposing this thinking onto your spiritual growth? Try as you may, you will be singularly unsuccessful at changing your heart. Only God can do that. But He wants you to play your part—setting the stage! So if you were the stage manager in a drama, would the director praise or criticize you for what you had done in this matter?

Planting It Deep

"Then will the eyes of the blind be opened
  and the ears of the deaf unstopped.
Then will the lame leap like a deer,
  and the mute tongue shout for joy.
Water will gush forth in the wilderness
  and streams in the desert." (Isaiah 35:5-6)

Praying It In

O Lord,
I seem to be
only just
inside Your door—a Christian
by the skin of my teeth!
Because the changes
in my life
are not dramatic,
nobody knows
I'm any different
from others.
Could it be that I am trying
to do it all myself?
If so, Lord,
show me the futility
of my efforts.
Fill me afresh
with Your Spirit,
and do the job properly!
Amen.

THE LIKENESS WILL BE UNMISTAKABLE

42

*"But we all, with unveiled face beholding as in a mirror
the glory of the Lord, are being transformed into the same image
from glory to glory, just as from the Lord, the Spirit."*
(2 Corinthians 3:18, NASB)

The change will not only be certain, but also recognizable! "We all . . . are being transformed into the same image." What image does the writer speak of? The image of whatever you are gazing at and filling your mind with. The likeness stamped upon you will be that of the object you are contemplating.

Spend five years with selfish people and, but for the grace of God, you'll become selfish. Spend five years with lazy people and yet again, but for the grace of God, you will become lazy. Spend five years gazing upon God and, now *because* of the grace of God, you will become godly! That principle remains unchanged. "The more I contemplate God the more I shall become like him."

Impressed upon the film of your life will be the image of whatever the camera of your mind is facing when you press the button of your quiet time. If you want a photo of your house, but then, camera in hand, turn your back on your house and press the button, you will get a picture of the house across the street. "But I didn't want a picture of the neighbor's house," you complain. "I wanted a picture of ours." The answer will surely come back, "Then you should have turned to face the right direction."

Obvious though such an answer is, many miss the point when it comes to applying that principle to the spiritual. "I want to be like Jesus," we say, "that people will know I'm a Christian." If we then turn our minds continually to soap operas or motorbikes, to the pursuit of wealth or the pursuit of women, we are going to reflect not Christ, but whatever we have used our minds to think about. For while we are not what we think we are, what we think—we are!

Where does your mind go when it is free to think or daydream? If you seriously think through these questions, then adjust your priorities, you will be more likely to board the right train and reach your desired destination.

David, who, as we saw, had a thirst after God which was second to none, teaches us another lesson in Psalm 27:4. He says, "One thing I ask of the LORD, *this is what I seek:* that I may dwell in the house of the LORD all the days of my life, to gaze upon the beauty of the LORD and to seek him in his temple" (emphasis added).

He was single-minded about getting to know God. His prayer was focused on just one thing. But he also actively pursued it. He loved the presence of the Lord and longed to gaze upon His beauty.

If that is what mainly preoccupies our thoughts, it will not be long before we will become like Jesus Christ. There are many ways to describe that likeness, but there are three New Testament portraits of a Christian which I like to combine: The Beatitudes, the fruit of the Spirit and the by-products of love.

The Beatitudes in Matthew 5 list lowliness or humility, mourning over sin, meekness, hungering and thirsting for righteousness, mercy, purity of heart and peacemaking. Add to these the fruit of the Holy Spirit in Galatians 5:22-23. These nine words—love, joy, peace, patience, kindness, goodness, faithfulness, gentleness and self-control—are in fact a description of the life of Jesus Christ which He longs to see growing as fruit in us. The third list is in First Corinthians 13:4-7, where we find fourteen ways in which a Christian should exhibit Christ's love.

Within these three passages, we have a fairly comprehensive description of what a real Christian should be. How I long that my life would constantly exhibit these qualities. For I know that it can! It comes about by gazing at the One who is the very personification of them all—Jesus!

The late Ralph Shallis, veteran missionary to Algeria and France, stayed in our home a year or two before he died. Our children said they could not recall having met anyone who reminded them more of what they understood Jesus to be like. It was not long before they found out why. Ralph not only tithed his money. He also tithed his time, giving a tenth of it each day for worship and contemplation. For two and a half hours each morning he would shut himself away and gaze upon God. No wonder he came to resemble Jesus!

Thinking It Through

I find it worthwhile keeping tabs on myself. Where are my interests? What is my first love? What is it I enjoy reading? Does it help or hinder my spiritual life? Ask yourself these questions for a week. You may get some surprises which will motivate you into change. After all, we become what we think!

Planting It Deep

"O LORD, you have searched me
*   and you know me.*
You know when I sit and when I rise;
*   you perceive my thoughts from afar.*
You discern my going out and my lying down;
*   you are familiar with all my ways.*
Before a word is on my tongue
*   you know it completely, O LORD." (Psalm 139:1-3)*

Praying It In

O Lord,
I thought
I was getting
away with it.
My reputation
far outweighs
my character!
People think
more highly of me
than they should.
But You knew me all along.
You saw through my masks.
The problem is
I knew I wasn't fooling You.
I just didn't want
to think about it.
O Lord, You are so patient.
I really do want to change,
but it's taking so long!
Amen.

THE PROCESS WILL BE GRADUAL

43

*"But we all, with unveiled face beholding as in a mirror
the glory of the Lord, are being transformed into the same image
from glory to glory, just as from the Lord, the Spirit."*
(2 Corinthians 3:18, NASB)

Beware of the overnight wizards—those who claim to bring about radical change with one wave of a wand. They'll shortchange you! Spiritual transformation is not something sudden but gradual. It is "from glory to glory," or from one degree of splendor to another.

Of course it may very well start with a crisis; it often does. But we must keep on reminding ourselves in these pages that a crisis not followed by a process becomes an abscess! The crisis of Christian conversion not followed by the process of sanctification will immunize us against further work by the Holy Spirit. The transformation of a son of Adam into the likeness of Christ is a lifelong process—and then some!

The transfer from Satan's kingdom to Christ's is immediate upon my repentance and faith, but the change into a holy lifestyle comes gradually. Each day another part of me will be cut or polished as I yield to the Master's hand and respond to each new flash of light from the prism of God's glory.

Lapel pins from one popular seminar read, "Please Be Patient: God's Not Finished with Me Yet!" How true! If God had finished working on me—even after these fifty years—I would be very disappointed. There are too many rough edges on this diamond. I want it polished and sparkling.

When God wraps up this age and believers are changed into Christ's likeness, "then shall I know fully." Until then "we see but a poor reflection as in a [polished metal] mirror" (1 Corinthians 13:12). In such mirrors we see but "darkly" (KJV), literally in an "enigma." Now we "know in part" but then "face to face." Exactly what we shall see is not spelled out, but we know it will include a fuller vision of God Himself than I can get even in my solitude.

Scripture tells us there is a sense in which God cannot be seen. "No one has ever seen God" (John 1:18). He is "invisible" (1 Timothy 1:17); He "dwells in unapproachable light; whom no man has seen or can see" (6:16, NASB).

We cannot even approach, much less enter that light. "If such infinite light is God's habitation, what must God Himself be?" asks Lenski. "This unapproachable light is uncreated, eternal and not the light called into being on the first day (Genesis 1). 'Whom no man has ever seen or can see' indicates that both fact and possibility are equally denied."[1]

Yet "blessed are the pure in heart; for they will see God" (Matthew 5:8). Our beholding God down here creates an insatiable appetite for Him. Our journey has only started. God will not disappoint. He fulfills every legitimate desire he plants in us. There, faith will give place to sight and we "shall see his face." But

> we will never be able to see or know all of God,
> for "his greatness is unsearchable" (Psalm
> 145:3). And we will not be able to see—at least
> with physical eyes—the spiritual being of God.

Yet Scripture says we will see God Himself.

We will be able to see the human nature of Jesus, of course. But it is not clear in exactly what sense we will be able to "see" the Father, the Holy Spirit, or the divine nature of God the Son. Perhaps the nature of this "seeing" will not be known to us until we reach heaven.

Although what we see will not be an exhaustive vision of God, it will be a completely true and clear and real vision of God. We shall see "face to face" and "we shall see him as he is"; his servants, we read, "shall see his face" (1 Cor. 13:12; 1 Jn. 3:2; Rev. 22:3-4).[2]

Down here the process of change comes gradually as we keep contemplating God. But at that time, when He breaks through the clouds, we shall see Him. And "when he appears, we shall be like him, for we shall see him as he is" (1 John 3:2). Only then will the transformation be complete. Our joy will be full!

Thinking It Through

If you have a cross-reference Bible, look up passages to see what we are told about heaven; especially about what spiritual beings will be like. Ask for humility as you do so, for "the secret things belong to the LORD our God" (Deuteronomy 29:29). Whatever we think heaven will be like, it will be a thousand times better.

Planting It Deep

"Then I saw a new heaven and a new earth, for the first heaven and the first earth had passed away, and there was no longer any sea. I saw the Holy City, the new Jerusalem, coming down out of heaven from God, prepared as a bride beautifully dressed for her husband. . . . [God] will wipe every tear from their eyes. There will be no more death, or mourning or crying or pain, for the old order of things has passed away." (Revelation 21:1-2, 4)

Praying It In

O Lord,
How grateful I am
for the foretaste of heaven
You give me on earth.
Sometimes
I sense Your presence
so close.
I simply cannot imagine
what Heaven itself will be like,
but I do so long
to be like You.
Remind me
to look out of my window
each morning and each night,
and say to myself
"Perhaps today!"
"Perhaps tonight!"
Amen.

GLORY IN! GLORY OUT!

44

*"But we all, with unveiled face beholding as in a mirror
the glory of the Lord, are being transformed into the same image
from glory to glory, just as from the Lord, the Spirit."*
(2 Corinthians 3:18, NASB)

Having spent much of my life in public speaking, I have learned the importance of communicating with my facial muscles as much as with my words. For this reason, where possible, I look for a spot where my face can be clearly seen by the audience.

To do this I often put up with being almost blinded by the very spotlight which will help me communicate. By the time my eyes have become adjusted to the brightness, the perspiration is dripping from my collar. Nobody has to convince me that if I want the light to be reflected off my face, I must stand facing that light. And if I am standing in the light, I never need ask whether my facial expressions can be seen. It is inevitable—they always are.

The more we gaze at Jesus, God's Light, the better we will reflect Him to a darkened world. But we will reflect that glory to no greater degree than we have absorbed it!

We saw earlier that our word "beholding" could be translated "mirroring." This then includes the reflecting mode as well as the beholding. But because "mirroring" is so ambiguous in English, you will recall I said translators struggle as to whether to translate it "beholding" or "reflecting."

But just as it is impossible to reflect what we do not behold, so will I surely reflect what I do behold.

We saw that our faces, like Moses', needed to be unveiled in order to behold and absorb. Similarly they will need to be unveiled so as to reflect Him to others. However, unlike Moses, who later covered his face so the fading of the glory would not be seen, we need have no such concern. The glory on his face was symbolic of the fading glory of the old covenant (Old Testament). It would come to an end, or fade. The new covenant (or New Testament) will never fade—it is the glory of Calvary! It is forever!

Years ago, when we lived in Montreal, we developed a regular habit. Just before 11 p.m., Rosemary would say to me, "Well, dear, it's time to watch the news." I would settle into a comfortable family room chair to see what in the world had happened.

She would head off to bed, and on her way upstairs, she would remind me to switch off the kitchen light. The news over, I dutifully obeyed instructions. But after switching off the light I would notice another light at the far end. The toaster and some cupboards were clearly visible. But where was the switch? There was none! It was the bright phosphorescent band across the kitchen wall telephone which visually yelled Fire! Police! Ambulance! and the numbers.

For four hours that little strip had been gazing at the kitchen light. When the room went dark, its role changed from a beholder to a reflector, casting light on all around it. But I've been down for an aspirin at 4 a.m. and it was hardly shining at all. Why? Because it had now gone four hours without contemplating that 100-watt bulb.

Similarly, the more we contemplate God, the more we become like Him.

Not merely in the words you say,
   Not only in your deeds confessed,
But in the most unconscious way
   Is Christ expressed.

Is it a beatific smile?
   A holy light upon your brow?
Oh no! I felt His presence
   When you laughed just now.

To me 'twas not the truth you taught,
   To you so clear, to me still dim;
But when you came you brought
   A sense of Him!

For from your eyes He beckons me,
   And from your heart His love is shed,
'Til I lose sight of you
   And see the Christ instead.[1]

Thinking It Through

How much does my life—not just my talking—reflect the likeness of Jesus? Am I willing to think this through? Then ponder how serious I really am about reflecting Him? Serious enough to do anything about it? If so, what?

Planting It Deep

"If the world hates you, keep in mind that it hated me first. . . . That is why the world hates you. Remember the words I spoke to you: 'No servant is greater than his master.' " (John 15:18-20)

Praying It In

O Lord,
the world's pull
is so strong!
I've tried to resist it,
and failed!
But You have overcome the world,
and You live within me!
Then work in me, Lord
So that
I too
will be victorious!
Amen.

A Prayer

O Lord,
this choice verse
has caused me to touch
the hem of Your garment.

Catching this glimpse of You
Has made me thirsty for more.

I now see
that there is
so much more to behold
than I have ever imagined.

I can hardly wait to know You better
and learn
how to abide in You.

I keep saying
that time is the problem,
but I honestly think
it's more my stubborn will.

Lord, let this desire
grip me and not let me go.
Give me no rest
until I have fixed my mind
and disciplined myself
to keep my appointments
with You.

Then teach me,
with barriers removed,
to gaze on Your lovely face
without distraction.

As the minutes pass into hours,
make me scarcely conscious of the time.
May the joy and ecstasy
of each moment gazing
be translated
into a life
which brightly reflects the glory of my King.
Amen.

My glorious Victor, Prince divine,
Clasp these surrendered hands in Thine;
    At length my will is all Thine own,
    Glad vassal of a Saviour's throne.

My Master, lead me to Thy door;
Pierce this now willing ear once more:
    Thy bonds are freedom; let me stay
    With Thee, to toil, endure, obey.

Yes, ear and hand, and thought and will,
Use all in Thy dear slav'ry still!
    Self's weary liberties I cast
    Beneath Thy feet; there keep them fast.

Tread them still down; and then I know
These hands shall with Thy gifts o'erflow;
    And pierced ears shall hear the tone
    Which tells me Thou and I are one.[2]

PART FIVE

Yielding

Romans 12:1-2

[1]I urge you therefore, brethren, by the mercies of God,to present your bodies a living and holy sacrifice,acceptable to God, which is your spiritual service of worship. [2]And do not be conformed to this world, but be transformed by the renewing of your mind, that you may prove what the will of God is, that which is good and acceptable and perfect. (NASB)

Leap Before You Look!

45

*"I urge you therefore, brethren, by the mercies of God,
to present your bodies a living and holy sacrifice,
acceptable to God, which is your spiritual service of worship.
And do not be conformed to this world, but be transformed
by the renewing of your mind, that you may prove
what the will of God is, that which is good and acceptable
and perfect." (Romans 12:1-2, NASB)*

I magine yourself in church on Sunday morning. The pastor begins his sermon with, "How many of you are willing to do what I teach this morning?" He waits. Things get quiet. The congregation thinks it's a trick. They wait for him to spell it out.

He continues, "I shall preach on a text from the Bible. How many of you will do it?" A handful of "spiritual" people, looking around, cautiously slip up an index finger.

Not satisfied, he adds, "This passage cannot be misunderstood. So how many of you will do what it says?" A few more slowly slip up their hands—halfway!

"Who is waiting until I tell you what I'll teach?" There's a cheer. Every hand goes up!

"All right," he says, "turn to Romans 12:1-2." The pages rustle. Folk whisper, still not sure what he has up his sleeve. But the truth will soon dawn!

He reads, then adds, "This passage is a clear biblical statement on how to know and enjoy God's will. There are two steps. First I present myself to God, willing to do whatever He wants. Second, if I trust Him without knowing the details, He guarantees I'll be shown His will and find it tremendously enjoyable."

"In God's economy," he adds, *"believing* is seeing! That's why I asked if you were willing to leap before you looked!"

That incident really happened. I was the preacher!

Ecstasy of communion with God is a means, not an end. It must lead to a desire to know God's will and live a godly life. Our passage gives clear direction to that end. Because God's will includes all the Bible, it should not matter which page. Before knowing where to turn, we should be able to tell God we are willing to do what He asks.

This ensures we will get more light as we read on. The condition "if any man is willing to do His will" (John 7:17, NASB) is as much a condition for getting insight as for knowing the source of Christ's words (the teaching of that verse). The one willing to do what God says will grasp God's will in a way the less willing cannot. We may well make a blanket statement of our willingness to obey, but cringe when we read the passage. That's being selective. Commit first—details later! That is what our verses are about!

By way of caution, this is the way God wants us to respond to *Him,* as our Lord. It is unwise to blankly commit our will to another person's conscience. Even Jesus was careful not to say yes to such a request (see Mark 10:35-36). We should weigh each demand made upon us. I must admit my wife would be an exception. Years of living together and observing her godly lifestyle gives me confidence she would never ask me to do what was contrary to Scripture. But beyond her—as humans go—I would have to think twice!

But when it comes to God, we cannot lose! For the promise which follows (Romans 12:2) says we will not only know, but test and enjoy the will of God (double meaning). Some Bible promises are unconditional. Others, like this one, are conditional. If we are thirsty to do God's will, we must meet those conditions.

The *crisis* in the first verse is followed by the *process* in the second. Verse 1 is a point of commitment; verse 2 is our ongoing life with God. There are five key words in our two verses, one in the first *(present)* and four in the second *(conformed, transformed, renewing, prove)*. We shall move through them in sequence to learn these wonderful truths about God's will.

Thinking It Through

Why not set yourself seven days to try this principle out. See whether it is true that we pick and choose what we will obey. Pray that God will open your eyes—to see that *all* His will is good. Then you will be willing to bow in prayer before opening your Bible and say: "Lord, I don't know what today's passage teaches, but I am willing to commit myself to doing it, simply because I know it is Your will for my life."

Planting It Deep

"Whoever has my commands and obeys them, he is the one who loves me. He who loves me will be loved by my

Father, and I too will love him and show myself to him." (John 14:21)

Praying It In

O Lord,
it is true!
I am selective
when it comes
to obeying You.
It wasn't my intention,
but I now see
I've been playing the game
of partial obedience.
Give me
a new desire
to be willing to do
not only the things I enjoy,
but also
those parts of Scripture
which make me
feel uncomfortable.
For I know
that in the end
those are
the very parts
that will become
my comfort.
Amen.

PRESENTING MY BODY

46

"I urge you therefore, brethren, by the mercies of God, to present your bodies a living and holy sacrifice, acceptable to God, which is your spiritual service of worship." (Romans 12:1-2, NASB)

To give to God that which I treasure most—my body—cannot but lead me to the place of blessing. Yet my stubborn, rebellious will resists the appeal. Only the Spirit of God, by the persuasive grace of God, can bring me to that place of submission.

The essence of Paul's exhortation is built around the word "present." This first verse tells us *who* is to present (or "offer," NIV), *why* we present, *what* we present and *how* we are to present. Let's touch on the first three, then later on the fourth.

1. Who Is to Present?

Paul is addressing his remarks to his "brethren" (not his Jewish brothers referred to in the third person in chapters 9-11, but his Christian brothers in Rome). He exhorts these believers to present their bodies. I must therefore conclude that it is possible to be a Christian but never to have presented my body to God. We will see later just what this means, but for now it is good to realize these verses apply to me, even though I may be a Christian.

2. Why Are We to Present?

The reason, the apostle says, is because of "the mercies of God." He has spent all the preceding chapters telling us of the mercies of God toward us in wooing, forgiving, redeeming and giving us victory in Christ. If anything will make us want to respond in sacrificial living, it is thinking about these great truths, particularly their focal point, the cross of Christ.

What is urged is not a please-offering but a thank-offering. We love not so He will love us more, but because He first loved us (1 John 4:19).

There are usually good motives on the part of organizations which offer a book or CD to those who will send a gift to the ministry. But there are also dangers. Without realizing it, they can be inculcating less-than-biblical habits in the practice of giving. Ephesians 1:3 tells us God has already given all spiritual blessings in Christ. And you cannot add more to all. As He has withheld nothing—even His only Son—from us, so we are to withhold nothing from Him. We are to give purely out of a thankful spirit.

3. What Are We to Present?

We are told to present our "bodies." When I became a Christian, the Holy Spirit took up residence within my human spirit, flooding my inner being with the light of the knowledge of the glory of God. But I may have restricted His control to those "religious" parts of my life. My sensual appetites, thought life, will and emotions could still function as they did before. He now commands me in effect to "be filled with the Spirit," so that my body too will be placed under His sovereign control.

The real you is your inner self. You merely possess a body. Just think what it will take for the real you to present your body. Because a river can rise no higher than its source, the deep-down you who is to do the presenting, must also be committed. Therefore you are to present both yourself and your body; you are to give God all of your life. You are both the giver and the gift (as Jesus on the cross was both priest and sacrifice).

If this is still fuzzy or a new concept for you, it would be wise to take a short detour right now by reading Rabbit Trail #3. This explains what happens when a person first becomes a Christian, and what may still remain to be done. Reading it now will ensure that the next few chapters become much more meaningful to you.

Thinking It Through

It's been said, "If you give because it pays—it won't!" Ask God to help you examine your motives. Do you give to God (whether money, time, energy, or as here, your body) so you'll get something out of it? Write down a list of what God has given you in Jesus Christ (all spiritual blessings—Ephesians 1:3), then if you can do so, write at the bottom of the sheet, "Lord, the list is never-ending! I now say thank you by giving you my body—my life!"

Planting It Deep

"Again, the kingdom of heaven is like a merchant looking for fine pearls. When he found one of great value,

he went away and sold everything he had and bought it." (Matthew 13:45-46)

Praying It In

O Lord,
I remember
the story
of the monkey
with the clenched fist.
He held onto that nut
inside the jar!
He couldn't
get his hand out,
because
he was reluctant
to let go the nut!
Help me to see
that keeping my life
in my own hands
will mean
I deny myself
that ultimate fulfillment
which comes from
being willing to let go
and hand over to You!
Amen.

Dead and Alive

47

"Present your bodies a living and holy sacrifice,
acceptable to God, which is your spiritual service of worship."
(Romans 12:1-2, NASB)

Having considered the who, the why and the what of presenting we are now to consider the "how." I do hope you have read Rabbit Trail #3.

4. How Am I to Present?

We're given three directives. We are urged to give our bodies as a sacrifice, as true worship, and as an act of the will.

(a) I am to present my body as a sacrifice. It is to be a *living* sacrifice! "Sacrifice" here specifically means a "slain" sacrifice. An animal in the slaughterhouse, though alive, is as good as dead. This means whatever in me wants its own way I must reckon as dead. It will fight fiercely, but if it is dead, it cannot respond to sinful suggestion. That's just it—a living death! Or, better, "the crucified life" (see Galatians 2:20).

It is also to be a *holy* sacrifice, set apart exclusively for God. A holy day was originally a day set apart to worship Him. Then we changed the word to "holiday"—with the capital "I" in the middle, so it became mine—to waste or enjoy! But *this* holy sacrifice is God's alone!

Whereas a Christian is pronounced holy because of Christ, there should follow a correspondingly holy lifestyle, conforming to the image of Christ. You, the branch, so abide in Christ the Vine, that the sap of God's Holy Spirit will reproduce in you the life of Jesus.

Such a sacrifice is *acceptable*. A life set apart solely for God's purposes becomes well pleasing to Him.

(b) I am to present my body as true worship. "Your reasonable service" (Romans 12:1, KJV) is an inadequate translation. None would question that it is "reasonable," but the thought goes deeper. The word means something spiritual, from the depth of my rational being.

The word "service" has thirty-seven meanings (Oxford). One of these is "worship"—especially public worship. When we speak of the "morning service," we do not mean washing church windows, but attending "morning worship." So "spiritual worship" is a better rendering than "reasonable service"; it is something I wholeheartedly give to God.

(c) I am to present my body as an act of my will. The command "present!" is not used. Paul rather "urges" us. True Christians should not need coercion. "For he who does it not willingly, solely as a result of admonition, he is no Christian," says Luther.

A dead body (or slain sacrifice) cannot get "off the altar" and start life over. Similarly, we present our bodies only once. This is exactly what is implied by the tense of our word "present." But what if we have forgotten something? I once watched Charles Ryrie use a loose-leafed binder to illustrate this. It was most enlightening.

Suppose I have a binder with sentimentally treasured documents inside. I present it to you, my friend, as a gift. You accept it with gratitude. Months later I return with several other

221

sheets, and I say to you, "These sheets belong to you!" But you say "No, they're not mine! I've never seen them before!" But I insist: "When I gave you that binder, I thought all the sheets were in it. But yesterday I came across these. In my mind I gave you them months ago. So take them! They're yours!"

When you present your body you may be unaware of what this will entail. Later, as you see what is involved, you need not wonder whether you should give that too. You say: "This is yours, Lord; when I gave my all, this was included!"

That is the crisis in a nutshell. *Who presents?* Christians! *Why present?* As a thank-offering for Calvary! *Present what?* Our bodies, our very lives! *How do we present?* As a sacrifice, as true worship, and as a deliberate act of the will!

Thinking It Through

It is no easy thing to present my body to the Lord. I will need to think it through, for it will mean a radical change in my way of living. After all, if I tell God I will do things His way, not mine, I'm letting someone else run my life. There surely could not be a more costly gift than this. Only the person I love most in the world will ever get that gift. Is that God? Or myself?

Planting It Deep

"Then Joshua said, 'You are witnesses against your-selves that you have chosen to serve the LORD.'

" 'Yes, we are witnesses,' they replied.

" 'Now then,' said Joshua, 'throw away the foreign gods that are among you and yield your hearts to the LORD, the God of Israel.'

"And the people said to Joshua, 'We will serve the LORD our God and obey him.' " (Joshua 24:22-24)

Praying It In

O Lord,
I've been thinking
about sacrifice.
Those who give up their lives
on a battlefield
give all,
but at least
there are no more battles!
What I find hard, Lord,
is this ongoing sacrifice,
day in, day out!
It's almost as radical
as letting You
make every decision.
But,
come to think of it,
that's exactly what it is!
O God, I need Your help!
Amen.

CRISIS AND PROCESS

48

*"I urge you therefore, brethren, by the mercies of God,
to present your bodies a living and holy sacrifice,
acceptable to God, which is your spiritual service of worship.
And do not be conformed to this world, but be transformed
by the renewing of your mind, that you may prove
what the will of God is, that which is good and acceptable
and perfect." (Romans 12:1-2, NASB)*

Starters and stickers usually find it hard to get along. Starters often shine in a crisis, like Romans 12:1, whereas stickers would prefer the steady plodding of 12:2.

Stickers find starters frustrating. They never seem to finish a job. They no sooner start than they lose interest and go off half-cocked to start something else, irresponsibly leaving the poor stickers to run with the ball.

Starters, on the other hand, find stickers dreadfully boring. "I can't believe you're still doing things that way," they say. No imagination. No innovation. No progress. Stuck-in-the-mud. I even heard one Christian leader say that if you are still doing the same things you were doing five years ago you have got to be passé (although I must admit I think that's taking it a bit too far!).

Simon Peter was a starter. John was a sticker. And they certainly had difficulty getting along. Do you remember that post-resurrection stroll across Capernaum beach? "What about him?" was Peter's question when John kept getting in his way (John 21:21). "None of your business," implied Jesus. "You get on with your own life and leave John to me" (see 21:22).

But see them after Pentecost (two pages over in my Bible), now filled with the Holy Spirit. "Now Peter and John went up *together* into the temple at the hour of prayer" (Acts 3:1, KJV, emphasis added). What a difference the Spirit makes!

Though unlikely to see eye to eye, starters and stickers usually make the best combination. Whether business partners, husbands and wives or evangelists and teachers, they need each other. Take one away and you lose either your creativity or your stability.

A crisis usually makes better news than a process! Ask any journalist! Yet stability in a society comes largely from the ongoing discipline and plodding of "the process." We have a parallel in our two verses. Romans 12:1, the crisis, will bring more amens and hallelujahs from the right kind of congregation. Everyone soon hears when a mediocre life is "rededicated to Christ." It is more dramatic, something we know actually happened.

But from half a century observing Christians I am convinced it is 12:2, the process, which will produce stability in the Christian life. Of course, it takes a crisis to trigger it. But while the crisis is essential, it is the process described here which will enable me to know, put to the test and approve this will of God with a sense of joy and fulfillment.

By nature, I'm a starter. I can't begin to tell you how many projects I've started and never finished. My wife Rosemary is a definite sticker. A plodder! As dependable as bed-rock. But we sure need each other, as starters and stickers usually do.

But when it comes to thirsting after God in order to have a life increasingly pleasing to Him, both stickers and starters just have to change—not giving up something, but adding something. Starters (12:1 crisis people) must get involved in the process of 12:2. That's not easy for them! And the patiently-waiting-for-it process people must trigger things off by an act of their will, responding to 12:1.

Of course, God continues to use our particular personality types. Even though we must all be involved in both verses, the starter is more likely to be able to nudge the sticker to get moving; but the daily prodding from there on will surely land in the sticker's lap. That's because this process described in 12:2 goes on for a lifetime. Starters are simply not allowed to leave that on the shelf and go start something else.

Thinking It Through

Do you find more difficulty starting a letter or finishing one? Deciding to move, or maintaining the old house? Are you more at home in Romans 12:1 or 12:2? When it comes to being a committed Christian, whichever part you favor, you're going to have to work on the other. The question is "Will you?" Ponder it well. How?

Planting It Deep

"But you, dear friends, build yourselves up in your most holy faith and pray in the Holy Spirit. Keep your-

selves in God's love as you wait for the mercy of our Lord Jesus Christ to bring you to eternal life. . . .

"To Him who is able to keep you from falling and to present you before his glorious presence without fault and with great joy—to the only God our Savior be glory, majesty, power and authority, through Jesus Christ our Lord, before all ages, now and forevermore! Amen." (Jude 20-21, 24-25)

Praying It In

O Lord,
I have so often
given up what I started.
I meant well
but miserably failed.
I've lost confidence
in my own feeble resources.
But I realize
it's at such times as this
that I've turned to You.
I now ask You again
to give me
the grace
of perseverance,
knowing that You
are the One
who is able to keep me
from falling.
Amen.

YEAST OR PLAY-DOH?

49

⚜

"And do not be conformed . . . but be transformed." (Romans 12:2)

The moment you present your body to God you become the object of a concentrated attack. The three archenemies of the Christian—the world, the flesh and the devil—join forces and make every effort to redirect your intentions. Satan, *the infernal enemy,* will ensure that your fleshly lusts, *the internal enemy,* will cause you to be attracted by the bait of the world, *the external enemy.*

Your old nature, the body of sin, at which the satanic appeal is aimed, must be reckoned "crucified with Christ," so it will not respond to sin's overtures (do read Romans 6).

By an act of your will you must now cooperate with the Holy Spirit. You must insist you will not yield to the destructive demands of the enemy. Without God's help this is impossible, for fallen man persists in his tendency to evil. But the Holy Spirit knows your longing, and He will supply the power for victory at the point of temptation.

Unfortunately we often allow the pull of the world to so affect us that what is "dead" sits up in its coffin and starts running the show once more. The apostle evidently experienced the same problem and enlarges on it in Romans 7:14-25. He now gives us important instruction by telling us in verse 2, "Do not be conformed to this world, but be transformed."

I recall some months ago sitting at the kitchen table with one of my little grandsons, making strange-looking objects out of Play-Doh. They were supposed to resemble things he could see in the kitchen. One of these was a "loaf of bread" which had obviously bulged its way over the top of the pan.

As I helped him squeeze and shape it with my fingers, I recall thinking about this verse and the well-known J.B. Phillips translation of it: "Don't let the world around you squeeze you into its own mold, but let God remold your minds from within."

Pursuing that imagery will enable us to grasp the crucial difference between these two words in verse 2, "conformed" and "transformed."

Imagine "conformed" as a loaf of bread made with Play-Doh. Its shape is determined entirely by the pressure from the outside. This is what the world succeeds in doing with our lives. It exerts such pressure, often peer pressure, to make us conform to the presuppositions on which it forms its opinions and priorities. It also urges us to use the props non-Christians lean on when they are lonely or helpless. We are guided from outside rather than from inside.

We are therefore told here, "Do not be conformed to this world," that is, "don't be squeezed by the spirit of this age!"

Also imagine "transformed" to be a loaf of bread made with yeast. (It tastes much better!) The shape of this loaf is not determined by pressure from outside, but by power from inside.

Whereas yeast in the Bible is mostly a symbol of evil, it is not always so. In Matthew 13:33 Jesus said, "The kingdom of heaven is like yeast that a woman took and mixed into a large amount of flour until it worked all through the dough." Here, yeast is a symbol of growth. Just as yeast permeates a batch of dough, fermenting it, so the Holy Spirit, by the Word, causes the principles of the kingdom of heaven to be spread right through a believer's life.

You must therefore allow the indwelling Spirit's shaping power to radiate out from your center and work its way right through you. He will then control your body the same way He is controlling your spirit. This is being "filled" with the Spirit (Ephesians 5:18).

It is one thing to know you must be transformed, but quite another to understand the way God's Spirit will do it. This process, called the "renewing of your mind," is perhaps the forgotten key to spiritual transformation. What in the world does it involve?

We shall soon see!

Thinking It Through

Active and passive Christianity can both be right, or both be wrong! If you either initiate your own ideas (active), or are controlled by worldly people (passive), your life will be counter-productive to godliness. On the other hand, if you ask God's Spirit to energize your mind and will (active) or be on the receiving end of His instructions (passive), you will be obeying the Bible.

Planting It Deep

"So Joshua fought the Amalekites as Moses had ordered, and Moses, Aaron and Hur went to the top of the hill. As long as Moses held up his hands, the Israelites were winning, but whenever he lowered his hands, the Amalekites were winning. . . . So Joshua overcame the Amalekite army with the sword." (Exodus 17:10-11, 13)

Praying It In

O Lord,
I know a river
cannot rise
any higher
than its source.
So when that source
is myself or others
from down here,
I can expect problems!
Lord, would You take over?
Be my Source
and my Resource,
and by Your Spirit
energize and control
my life,
so I'll become
a transformed person.
Amen.

RENEWING MY MIND

50

❦

"Be transformed by the renewing of your mind."
(Romans 12:2)

It is clear from this part of our verse that the mind controls the body as a steering wheel controls a car. If the Bible is the map, your life is the car and your mind the steering wheel, the car will go in the direction the wheel is turned.

Because you have presented your body to God, the Holy Spirit should now be the driver of the car of your life. His hands are on the steering wheel of your mind. He does not replace your mind, but influences it to godly living.

Notice that this does not destroy but enhance your freedom. Birds were made to fly and fish to swim. They are not free unless they can do that. Christian freedom is not freedom to think your own thoughts, but freedom to think God's thoughts. You are not truly free as long as you cannot think God's thoughts. Satan's job is to ensure you won't.

Although the Holy Spirit should be driving, the "old man," your old selfish fleshly nature, is in the back seat. Since his license to control you was taken away (Romans 12:1), he seems more determined than ever to grab the steering wheel. He knows that if he controls your mind, he will control your life.

This is why it is imperative that you make the Holy Spirit the only licensed Driver; He alone can cause you to think God's thoughts and go on renewing your mind. And what you think, you become! A Christ-filled mind leads to a Christ-filled life.

Renewing the mind is a concept similar to repentance. We have already seen that our English word "repent" means "to think again." The implication is that you have a "change of mind" (the Greek word). God enables you to change your value system so that you "seek first the kingdom of God and His righteousness."

We sometimes wrongly limit "repentance" to initial conversion. Although "renewing" is a different word, the thought is similar, with perhaps a greater emphasis on moral change. For you must go on repenting; you must go on changing your mind. It is a process, not a once-only affair.

This process of renewing would be called, in computer language, deprogramming and reprogramming. We must choose to reject the old principle by which our unregenerate minds were programmed and replace it with a biblical principle.

For example, Paul says, "Be renewed in the spirit of your mind, and put on the new self which in the likeness of God has been created in righteousness and holiness of the truth" (Ephesians 4:23-24, NASB). Eight verses then follow with four things we must deprogram from our minds and four things we must use to reprogram or replace them.

De-Program	*Re-Program*
Laying aside falsehood (v. 25)	Speak truth (v. 25)
Steal no longer (v. 28)	Let him labor (v. 28)

No unwholesome words (v. 29)	Words good for edification (v. 29)
Put away bitterness (v. 31)	Be kind one to another (v. 32)

Paul speaks elsewhere (2 Corinthians 10:5) of "bringing into captivity every thought to the obedience of Christ." That is, in essence, what we do as we renew our minds.

I may, for example, think too highly of myself—clearly an unscriptural attitude (Romans 12:3). The Holy Spirit then takes the butterfly net of my will, captures my thoughts of vanity, bringing them into obedience to Christ by changing my mind on the matter. In this way, my renewed mind grows to "think God's thoughts after Him."

So renewing my mind is an ongoing process. Having been a Christian for nearly fifty years, I would hope that by now at least ninety percent of the decisions I make are according to biblical principles rather than the way a non-renewed mind thinks. But if I think the process is complete, I'd better think again.

Thinking It Through

If your mind were a compass, it would be unreliable until properly set! The unregenerate mind is like that. You must insist on setting yours by the Bible (God's plumb line, God's level, true north). Try putting into brief principles some of the lessons you learn as you read it. Then plant them firmly into your mind, ready for action when they're needed.

Planting It Deep

"My soul is consumed with longing for your laws at all times. . . . Your word is a lamp to my feet and a light for my path." (Psalm 119:20, 105)

Praying It In

O Lord,
I sure live
in an upside-down world!
It seems
all my tendencies
are the opposite
of your will.
I need deprogramming, Lord,
to allow your Spirit
the freedom to work.
As I read
Your wisdom book,
the Bible,
I now give You permission
to reprogram
my mind
aright,
knowing that this alone
will bring true freedom.
Amen.

THE ENJOYMENT OF DOING GOD'S WILL

51

"That you may prove what the will of God is,
that which is good and acceptable and perfect." (Romans 12:2)

Some Christians are governed by a crisis theology. They go from crisis to crisis rarely thinking of what happens in between. Others have a process theology. They'd like the process to go on but have never triggered it by unconditionally yielding their will to God.

You first present your body to God, once and for all. Then you choose to have your mind renewed day by day. The result of crisis and process is the kind of transformation that causes you to discover, put to the test, and approve what the will of God is. But how does it work?

Before the crisis, when God showed you His will, you may have cringed. It sounded distasteful because your mind still thought according to the standards of the world. But as your mind becomes more renewed, your reaction to God's will changes. Not only do you find it easier to discover His will (for the Holy Spirit empowers your mind), but you increasingly agree with what God shows you. You say, "That's great, God!" really meaning, "That's exactly the way I see it!"

It is not that God has "come around" to your way of thinking, but that you have come around to God's. The more the

Holy Spirit reprograms your mind with Scriptural principles, the more God's will becomes delightful and enjoyable. That's because Scriptural principles and God's will are the same!

Whereas before, you were apprehensive to ask what God's will was, now you become open to it. You are even eager to ask, because you are finding more and more that you like what He says. In this way you show you are in process of being changed. Spiritual transformation is taking place. Like the caterpillar changing into a butterfly, you are entering a new dimension of Christian living. You are flying instead of crawling.

In its conclusion, Romans 12:2 tells us three things about the will of God:

1. God's will is good. There are times when, because we "see through a mirror, darkly" (literally, "enigmatically") we question God. Something happens in our lives and we cannot see how God can be good. But it is we who are short-sighted. For God can see the big picture and often allows a problem to prevent a bigger one. Of one thing we can be sure. God is always good; sometimes we recognize it (particularly when things go our way), and sometimes we don't. But whether we recognize it or not, He is always good!

2. God's will is perfect. God always takes every detail into account. Because you do not know what is going to take place in your life five years down the road (or even tomorrow!), you will find it difficult to understand why this or that takes up your time or causes you "unnecessary" trouble. Hindsight's 20-20 vision may later let you see the reasons why (not always!). But God longs for you to trust Him now, even before faith gives way to sight. And "as for God, his way is perfect" (Psalm 18:30).

3. God's will is acceptable. Such a will is already acceptable from God's viewpoint (the main thought) but it now also becomes acceptable to you, because your mind is in harmony with God's. You can say with the psalmist, "How sweet are your words to my taste, sweeter than honey to my mouth!" (Psalm 119:103).

The fact that the same word "acceptable" occurs in verse 1 is significant. There, your life is to be made acceptable (or well-pleasing) to God. Here God's will is something that will become acceptable (or well-pleasing) to you. So in a nutshell: "When my life becomes acceptable to God [v.1], God's will becomes acceptable to me [v. 2]."

To the degree that is happening in your life, you are becoming a transformed person. Then, and only then, will you be willing to "leap before you look."

Thinking It Through

Could there possibly be anything more pleasing than knowing that God and you are on the same wavelength; that His thoughts are increasingly becoming your thoughts? You will want to do what He wants, not just from duty, but because you love Him and you think the same way. God's will becomes second nature (or is that first-nature?) to you. Well, we can be like this. But it takes time. Lots of it. Are you ready?

Planting It Deep

"But his delight is in the law of the LORD, and on his law he meditates day and night. He is like a tree planted by streams of water, which yields its fruit in season and whose leaf does not wither. Whatever he does prospers." (Psalm 1:2-3)

Praying It In

O Lord,
I admit that
I have sometimes found
the Christian life
a drag!
Usually, it was when
I did not want
to do your will.
Give me, I pray,
such a delight in Your Word
that I will soak it up
until I am saturated
like a sponge
with Your desires.
For I know that spells
D-E-L-I-G-H-T!
Amen.

PART SIX

Searching

Proverbs 2

¹*My son, if you accept my words*
  and store up my commands within you,
²*turning your ear to wisdom*
  and applying your heart to understanding,
³*and if you call out for insight*
  and cry aloud for understanding,
⁴*and if you look for it as for silver*
  and search for it as for hidden treasure,
⁵*then you will understand the fear of the* LORD
  and find the knowledge of God.
⁶*For the* LORD *gives wisdom,*
  and from his mouth come knowledge and
    understanding.

THIRSTING AFTER WISDOM

52

"For the LORD gives wisdom, and from his mouth come knowledge and understanding." (Proverbs 2:6)

A braham Lincoln once said, "I have been driven many times upon my knees by the overwhelming conviction that I had nowhere else to go. My own wisdom and that of all about me seemed insufficient for that day."[1]

The purpose of cultivating a thirst after God is not just so we will feel good. It is to enable us to live a godly life. Our minds, constantly being renewed, need now to be filled with God's wisdom so we will know how to act in any given situation.

We are about to embark on a journey of discovery. Taking the rich language of Proverbs 2:1-6, we are going to see in our next few segments how to draw the water of God's wisdom out of the well of Scripture. As we learn to study the Bible, it is not for the enhancing of reputation but for the shaping of character.

Each time we open the Bible we should thank God for those who over the centuries have given their lives, many burned at the stake, so we can soak ourselves in the Word in our own language.

Every verse of this Proverbs passage breathes, even pants with longing and thirst. But the prime motivation is not a subjective sense of ecstasy. Being "carried away" by the Spirit in ecstatic rapture (something I admit I enjoy!) may well give a temporary high. But unless such euphoria is followed by an increasingly righteous lifestyle, it avails little except to keep a person hooked on God until the next high.

The psalmist knew that, and his cry in Psalm 119:20 could well be the text on which our passage is the commentary: "My soul is consumed with longing for your law at all times."

The more we get to know God, the more we become familiar with His thinking, His ways, His choices—what He likes and what He abhors. God's choices are the always-good decisions He makes because He is all wise. As we grow in the knowledge of Him, these gradually become our decisions too. We get to understand His mind. His wisdom becomes ours, His choices ours. Such pursuit ensures a richer communion with the One after whom we thirst.

Proverbs 2 shows the route we must travel if our search for true wisdom is to be fruitful. It assures us that as we search, the author, God, will ensure we find it. There is no better way to get to know God!

The wise counsel of our verses was likely given by a Hebrew father to his son. But as this is God's inspired Word, we can justifiably accept this counsel as addressed from our heavenly Father to us, His children.

Because this is Hebrew poetry, some basic principles will help our understanding.

First, the Book of Proverbs uses different words to describe wisdom (like knowledge, insight or understanding). Whereas elsewhere we may need to know the subtle differences, it is not so crucial here. Proverbs tends to use the words as synonyms, much like Psalm 119 repeatedly uses eight words to describe Scripture.

Secondly, you will notice that the second line of each verse says basically the same as the first but in different words. This is intentional and is one of the main forms of Hebrew poetry, where it is the concepts rather than the words that rhyme. (Proverbs also has other kinds of parallelism, where lines are opposites or complementary. See 10:1 and 14:7 as respective examples).

Thirdly, in addition, verses 1 and 2 go further still. The second line of each seems to go one stage beyond the first. It takes the thought deeper. I have called this "intensified parallelism," and in these two verses only, we will treat that second line as a separate step.

Starting in our next segment, I want us to look particularly at the seven steps we see in verses 1 to 5 (verse 6 is more the reason than the process). Each of our steps centers around a verb and all seven of them will be useful pegs on which to hang our thoughts about milking the Bible for God's wisdom.

Translations differ more in these poetic books than any part of Scripture. So whereas I am using the New International Version (as above) you will find your own version, if different, helpful to keep at your side to give you extra insight.

Thinking It Through

To thirst after God is no purposeless mystical experience. It has a goal in sight. That we may live right and worship right. The satisfaction we get is no ethereal out-of-this-world feeling, but that of knowing God. That means at very least knowing God's wisdom. Why not stop now and check if your thirst for God is properly motivated?

Planting It Deep

"If any of you lacks wisdom, he should ask God, who gives generously to all without finding fault, and it will be given him." (James 1:5)

Praying It In

O Lord,
I have made
so many foolish decisions
in life.
Even though I cannot undo them,
I want to start over.
The wisdom I had
was earthly wisdom.
Now I must have Your wisdom,
the wisdom which is from above.
For knowing Your wisdom
means knowing Your ways,
and to know Your ways
is to know You.
I can hardly wait, Lord.
Amen.

ACCEPTING THE BIBLE
AS GOD'S INSPIRED WORD

53

STEP ONE: "If you accept my words . . ." (Proverbs 2:1)

"Accepting" is a word used frequently to describe our receiving from God's hand His free gift of salvation in Jesus Christ. Yet this word, which became more popular in the last hundred years, visibly irked A.W. Tozer. He saw it as the verbal culprit in reducing the experience of God from a lifelong process to a momentary decision.

He often expressed his dislike for the concepts it conjured up, especially that of reluctant condescension. It's as if we said to God, "Well, I've thought it through and I guess I've nothing much to lose. I may as well turn the key, lift the latch and let you in. But please be sure to stay in your room because I don't want you interfering in my life." Such reasoning, he felt, did little more than get the "fanatics" off your back when asked if you had "accepted Christ."

Words often lose their punch by overuse. Yet it is essential God's gift of salvation be "accepted" by us. Short of a futile effort to work our own way to heaven there is no alternative. We need to shout from the housetops that to "accept" Him means that He enters not as a servant at our beck and call, but as our Master and Lord.

248

Verse 1, however, speaks not about accepting Christ but "accepting" the Bible. Our Father urges us to accept His words. For in addition to "accepting Christ," I need to consciously accept the Scriptures as God's inerrant Word.

After becoming a believer, I spent hundreds of hours trying to satisfy myself that this Bible really was what it claimed to be. Thankfully I emerged one day from that time of heart-searching with greater conviction than ever that it was. Since that day half a century ago, I cannot recall even one time when I have questioned its inspiration (although I have often grieved over my failure to obey!).

That conclusion was not blind acceptance; I had done my homework. That judgment became a growing conviction. My honest search those years ago has paid rich dividends—particularly as I explain this truth to others.

My conviction has been a compelling incentive to spend many hours a day pondering Scripture. I would never otherwise be motivated to study the meaning of its words.

Four verses well worth remembering helped me see the value of pursuing God's wisdom in its smallest details (Matthew 24:35; John 10:34-36; Galatians 3:16; Matthew 5:18, respectively):

1. *The Whole Bible:* "Heaven and earth will pass away but my words will never pass away." This is Jesus' blanket stamp of authority on what He knew was Holy Writ.

2. *A Single Word:* Jesus answered the Jews, "Is it not written in your Law, 'I have said you are gods'? If he called them 'gods,' to whom the word of God came—and the Scripture cannot be broken—what about . . . ?" Jesus then builds an argument on a solitary word as final evidence. Each word the Holy Spirit chooses is important.

3. A Single Letter: The Apostle Paul confirms a major doctrine on the basis that "the Scripture does not say 'and to seeds' meaning many people, but 'and to your seed' meaning one person, who is Christ." A singular or plural ending makes a difference.

4. The Smallest Stroke: Jesus makes the amazing statement, "until heaven and earth disappear, not the smallest letter ("one jot," KJV), not the least stroke of a pen ("one tittle," KJV—a hardly visible stroke within a letter) will by any means disappear from the Law until everything is accomplished."

Have you merely accepted what you were told about the revelation and inspiration of Holy Scripture? Or did you thoughtfully read and consider it and come to that conclusion yourself? The best test of a tree is its fruit. And the fruit of changed lives is unquestionable. But for you to answer the honest questions of others, it would be valuable to read what the Bible says about its own inspiration and try to obtain a helpful booklet about its transmission. (I found great help in *The New Testament Documents: Are They Reliable?* by F.F. Bruce).

Thinking It Through

If Jesus had such a lofty view of Scripture, so must we. Perhaps you will shortly come to that place where you accept that what the Holy Spirit originally inspired is God's inerrant Word. Perhaps this prayer of dedication can become yours: "I unequivocally and irrevocably accept the teachings of the Bible, in their entirety, as Your inviolable Word, my standard for living my life. By Your grace I will never again doubt its source. I pray for an obedient spirit to practice its truth. Amen."

Planting It Deep

"All Scripture is God-breathed and is useful for teaching, rebuking, correcting and training in righteousness, so that the man of God may be thoroughly equipped for every good work." (2 Timothy 3:16)

Praying It In

O Lord,
You have given me
an enquiring mind.
I find it hard
to accept "facts"
without proof.
I'm like Thomas,
(I'm from Missouri,
the show-me-state).
But when it comes
to Scripture, Lord,
I have
Your own signature
that it is
what it claims to be.
From here on,
that should
be good enough for me.
May I never
question it again,
knowing it is has
passed Your test.
Amen.

STORING GOD'S WORD IN MY MIND

54

STEP TWO: "Store up my commands within you." (2:1)

I frequently meet "nominal evangelicals" who claim to have "accepted Christ" in the casual way discussed earlier, but who seem to have little interest in pursuing a Christian lifestyle.

Similarly, we can have a general acceptance of the Bible's inspiration and authority with little thought of letting it affect our minds and behavior. Unless we change, our lives will not count for much.

This second (parallel) line of verse 1 shows us how. It does seem to go further than the first: "Store up my commands within you." We must not only accept the Bible as God's inspired Word, but we must also store it up in our minds and memories.

The word "storing" used here means to hide (in my heart), to treasure, to protect from being stolen. Decades of observation and personal experience have shown me the immense value of memorizing parts of the Bible for frequent recall and enjoyment.

The difficulty of which translation to use has contributed to the decline in Bible memorization. (Anyone remember "sword drill"?) Despite this, those thirsty for God will find a way. And the younger we learn, the easier it will keep coming back—to encourage or haunt us—for the rest of our lives.

I have also found it useful to condense, each in a brief sentence, many timeless principles taught in Scripture. I call them my nutshells. So many are in my mind. I pull them off the shelf of memory and apply them at appropriate times in life. With such a simple memory aid I can remember biblical principles I may otherwise forget. Both the words of Scripture and these one-sentence principles are part of "storing" God's commands.

As I began my Christian life, I was determined to get to know the Bible. At age twenty, in Hong Kong, I had heard of the Navigators Bible memory system. It was not available in the colony in 1950, but my will provided the proverbial way. I cut up manila folders, typed a verse on one side of each of the small cards, with the reference on the other. I then made myself little pouches in which to carry them.

My work demanded I take the Star Ferry across Hong Kong harbor twice each day. I used the ten-minute crossing to memorize. After four months of persistence and reviewing, I had learned about 500 verses.

Thinking back over five decades, it is these verses, learned at an age when I was better able to absorb, that keep coming to my mind as I preach the Word.

I chose to learn those single verses which encapsulated some great truth of Scripture or brought encouragement to my heart. They could be recalled at various times of need and ministered great comfort. One month I memorized verses which challenged my commitment to the Lord; another time, verses which expressed hope in times of discouragement. Even when I was without my Bible or New Testament, I then found I could chew on these verses and ponder them as I traveled, as I waited for somebody or when doing some manual task which required little thinking effort.

I now wish I had learned consecutive verses or longer passages so I would be sure to think of the truths in their proper context. If I were to do it all over again I would start with passages like The Ten Commandments in Exodus 20, a few favorite psalms like 23, 51, 63 and 84. I would learn Isaiah 53 (the gospel according to Isaiah), the Beatitudes from Matthew 5, the love chapter in First Corinthians 13 and the literary masterpiece on the New Jerusalem in the King James Version of Revelation 21.

With such a diversity of passages, all well-known, I would be able to recall God's standards of holiness, the centrality of the cross, the way to get along with others, the hope of the Christian and especially those psalms which would draw out my heart to God.

But despite the aging process, it is never too late to start storing up Scripture. If it is true that "few Christians end well," this could be the God-sent antidote, ensuring that I mellow rather than become a wicked old man.

Thinking It Through

Why not keep a little notebook to jot down the references of verses you would like to memorize. Keep adding to the list, at the same pace you learn those already on it. Pick a version and stick to it. How about trying a short chapter by heart?

Planting It Deep

"But as for you, continue in what you have learned and have become convinced of, because you know those from whom you learned it, and how from infancy you have known the holy Scriptures, which are able to make you wise for salvation through faith in Christ Jesus." (2 Timothy 3:14-15)

Praying It In

O Lord,
I confess
there were many things
I never thought
I could do,
and yet did!
Give me
the determination
to press ahead
and learn Your Word,
before the hardening
of my memory
prevents it.
Amen.

TURNING MY EAR TO WISDOM

55

STEP THREE: "Turning your ear to wisdom." (2:2)

I mentioned a few segments back that Abraham Lincoln, who loved the Bible and knew it intimately, said: "I have been driven many times upon my knees by the overwhelming conviction that I had nowhere else to go. My own wisdom and that of all about me seemed insufficient for that day."[1]

Like Lincoln, you must choose to turn in the right direction to hear Wisdom's voice. When God's Holy Spirit has done a real work in your heart, you will long to know God better. Not just as a duty, but your first love, something you do whenever you are free to choose—and even sometimes when you are not.

I recall, on many afternoons when our children were infants, Rosemary suddenly leaving the kitchen and going into the hallway. She would stand at the bottom of the stairs and "incline her ear" for a few seconds. She had heard a cry or cough—or thought she had—and was going through the pre-monitor-days procedure to see if the baby was awake. This "inclining" is the meaning of our word.

For you to turn in the direction of God's wisdom means primarily that you choose to hear the words of the Bible. But in addition, God loves to provide other channels—older, godly, experienced Christians—who have walked life's pathway longer than you.

It was in such a search for wisdom that I first asked Dr. Tozer for a little of his time. Then, with my appetite whetted, I kept going back for more. One sure way to get a piece of a wise man's day is to show how hungry you are for God's wisdom.

Actually, most of those I learn from are younger than I, but—then again—that's to be expected when most people in general are younger. However, when opportunities come, I love to spend time with those in their eighties or nineties. They usually have so much to teach us about life. White hair does not always indicate great wisdom, but I am frequently delighted when I find that the "snow on the roof" has not replaced the fuel in the woodshed or the "fire in the furnace."

At thirty years old, I was deeply impressed by eighty-year-old hymnwriter Arthur Smith, whom I was driving to a conference in upstate New York. Although fifty years my senior, he kept asking my opinion on several matters. I learned from his sharing but I especially saw a great model of humility!

The other side of the coin is true too. Younger people need to take the initiative to learn from those who have experienced life. To answer questions is not a tiring chore for octogenarians. Many are too rarely asked their opinion—even on subjects where their knowledge excels. Overwhelmed that someone cares enough to ask, they grasp the opportunity with both hands and find themselves reminiscing and reveling in God's goodness in their past. I would have missed so much if I had not turned my ear to their wisdom over these decades. Try it out!

When I am at home between engagements, I rarely pass over an unfamiliar word in a book without enquiring about the meaning. Love of reading has given my wife a broad vocabulary and she can usually give me its sense. If she too is stumped, we usually go for the Oxford or Webster, find the meaning and origin, then firmly plant it in our minds. I do the same with biblical or theological terms which are new to me.

The best place to turn for wisdom is the Bible itself. All the important truths about life are right there. When, however, I cannot understand something, so plain and obvious to someone else, I "incline my ear" to them, listening intently and asking more questions where necessary. Such opportunities frequently occur during a conversation. When I hear something new to me, I usually ask for a rerun so I can learn. This also encourages those who have made the effort to share.

Thinking It Through

Do you set time aside each day to turn your thoughts to the Wisdom of the Word? And could you not make it a practice to follow some of the ideas discussed above? How will you do it? Why not ask some Christian senior citizens for an appointment to ask them to reminisce about the lessons they've learned from life? Decisions like these will bring you one step closer to being a wise person.

Planting It Deep

"Listen, my sons, to a father's instruction; pay attention and gain understanding. I give you sound learning, so do not forsake my teaching. When I was a boy

in my father's house, still tender, and an only child of my mother, he taught me and said, 'Lay hold of my words with all your heart; keep my commands and you will live. Get wisdom, get understanding; do not forget my words or swerve from them.' . . . Wisdom is supreme; therefore get wisdom. Though it cost all you have, get understanding." (Proverbs 4:1-5, 7)

Praying It In

O Lord,
I cringe
to think of
all the elderly people
I have taken for granted
and hardly passed
the time of day with.
Lord, I want to learn
from those who know You
and love Your Word,
and who have
borne the burden
and heat of the day.
Give me success, Lord,
and make me a wise person.
Amen.

APPLYING MYSELF TO DO IT

56

❦

STEP FOUR: "Applying your heart to understanding." (2:2)

While this line of the proverb reinforces the previous one, it also adds a further dimension—putting into practice what we learn. We'll need to look closely at each word.

To "apply" your heart means giving your all to the task at hand, your stimulus coming from deep inside you. By "heart," the author here seems to particularly emphasize the thinking process of the mind and decision-making capacity of the will. Furthermore, the word "understanding" in the writer's language does not mean merely grasping a concept, so as to pass an exam (as our English word can mean), but putting the concept into practice in life. In this sense, you cannot "understand" a chair without sitting on it!

We in the Western world have gradually reduced Christianity from a way of life to a statement of faith. Knowing has largely replaced doing. But the Hebrew concept of wisdom makes it inseparable from doing.

I have, on more than one occasion, suggested to a Sunday morning congregation that if they have no time to think about how to apply the message to life, they should skip church next Sunday to do so. Better to give time to applying what we know than accumulating even more unproductive information.

The more we know, the more strictly we shall be judged by God. Amassing knowledge to win arguments is dangerous. Falling into the habit of hearing without doing (or even thinking about) is extremely hard to reverse. Tozer often expressed his disgust at the common disease of substituting "the grasping of the concept" for "the experiencing of the reality."

To apply our hearts to understanding is the sure antidote. "For God," says John Stott, "will judge us, not by our 'credenda' (what we say we believe) but by our 'agenda' (what we do). Because we only really believe the things we do."[1]

Glubb Pasha, the Commander-in-Chief of the Arab Legion, wrote many books on Middle East military strategy. Before he died in the 1980s, he traversed Britain lecturing on "The Fate of Empires."

Picking up Toynbee's ideas, he observed that virtually every empire in the last three thousand years had lasted ten generations or about 250 years in its greatness. Pasha noted that the same successive stages were observable in all those we know about. Each empire passed through bondage, courage, conquering, sending pioneers then merchants. Each later entered an age of art and luxury. The money would often be left to educational institutions, thus increasing their size and number.

Each empire started with two or three universities, e.g., Oxford and Cambridge, or Harvard, Yale and Princeton, but ended with a university—or two—in each city.

But intellectual pursuits resulted in "knowing" taking over from "doing." This was always accompanied by a decline in morals. This moral depravity ultimately produced a passive population with little resistance being offered to ambitious conquerors.

Incidentally, those in the spotlight at the beginning of an empire were soldiers, pioneers and statesmen, while at the end of each empire the three at center-stage were always actors, athletes and musicians, with the stringed instrument always reappearing.

Note the thin end of the wedge. It was when knowing took over from doing! Naisbitt's *Megatrends* of some years ago showed that we in North America have passed from the manufacturing era to the information era—surely different words for the same repeated decline from "doing" to "knowing."

Perhaps nothing characterizes North American Christianity at present like the slide from living the life to merely knowing the facts. Therefore this fourth stage in our search for wisdom, while relevant to every nation, is especially urgent and crucial for North Americans.

Thinking It Through

If this problem of "knowing" taking over from "doing" is central to the decline in the quality of evangelical Christianity, have you contributed to it? Have you been sucked into the system? Can you help reverse it?

Planting It Deep

"Why do you call me 'Lord, Lord' and do not do what I say? . . . The one who hears my words and does not put them into practice is like a man who built a house on the ground without a foundation. The moment the tor-

rent struck that house, it collapsed and its destruction was complete." (Luke 6:46, 49)

Praying It In

O Lord,
for a long time
I have known
far more than I practice.
There are so many areas
of deficiency
that I am ashamed!
Each one
takes me further along
the road to hypocrisy!
Show me the steps to take
to reverse the trend.
Sting my conscience
with each inconsistency,
and help me change.
Amen.

CALLING FOR GOD TO SHOW ME

57

~❦~

STEP FIVE: "If you call out for insight." (2:3)

How wonderful that in our search for wisdom, God has put into His Word this short passage with the steps we must go through to obtain it. In this segment, we learn the indispensability of asking God to show Himself to us. We "call out for insight."

Without God's enlightening, even the most brilliant intellect is inadequate to grasp the deep truths of the Bible. "The man without the Spirit does not accept the things that come from the Spirit of God, for they are foolishness to him, and he cannot understand them, because they are spiritually discerned" (1 Corinthians 2:14). Our own passage says, "The LORD gives wisdom, from his mouth come knowledge and understanding" (Proverbs 2:6).

I recall, more than once, searching up and down a radio frequency band, unable to find a station I knew was broadcasting, only to realize I was trying to find an FM station on the AM band. Trying to understand the wisdom of God with the human intellect brings the same frustration. It's on a completely different wavelength—one simply not available to us until we invite Christ into our lives.

Once we yield to His overtures, God's Spirit takes up residence in our hearts, giving us the capacity to tune in to a frequency not previously accessible. If this is a new concept to you, you will find much help reading straight through all of First Corinthians 2. It gives great insight and takes very few minutes.

God, in His wisdom, has "hidden [certain] things from the wise and learned, and revealed them to little children" (Matthew 11:25). A swollen head or an infatuation with intellectual prowess is the greatest hindrance to knowing God. For without reverence and humility no one can ever comprehend His truth.

Having left school at fourteen because of wrong priorities, a craze for sport and putting undue pressure on my parents, I soon found I was not prepared to face life with any degree of competence. Six years later, having come to faith, I realized how foolish that earlier decision had been. But having committed myself to eight years in the Royal Air Force, I knew it was extremely unlikely I would ever return to school.

Following my conclusion that the Bible was indeed the Word of God (related earlier under our first word, "accepting"), I was one day reading this very passage in Proverbs 2.

Realizing I had neither the wisdom of this world nor the wisdom of God, I dropped to my knees and said something like: "Lord, I have just read your promise to give wisdom to those who long for it and who meet your conditions. I want to be saturated with your wisdom. I will apply myself to that pursuit. I ask right now that, as I play my part, you will give me what I long for."

As I look back, I realize that this is what is meant by "if you call out for insight and cry aloud for understanding." From around that time in my Christian life, I came to the realization that I was beginning to understand the meaning of many of the Scriptures I was reading. After all, God had promised to give insight.

I could hardly believe how I had for so long neglected such wonderful truths for a fulfilled life. How grateful I was that God drew me to Himself at twenty rather than at thirty.

Perhaps, as you read these pages, you too are realizing you have never got that serious with God and His Word. Could it be that this book has found its way into your hands because God knows this is your time? One thing is sure—God has already made His move, with both invitation and promise. The next move is up to you. What better time than now?

Thinking It Through

Imagine how difficult it would be if you were blind, never having had sight. What would come into your mind if someone tried to explain what trees or tulips were like? However good your imagination, nothing would come near having your eyes opened so you could see for yourself. When it comes to spiritual truth, Satan has blinded all our minds. Only Christ, by His Spirit, can open them. When He does, a whole new world is accessible to us. If He has opened your eyes, spend time thanking Him now.

Planting It Deep

"Jesus declared, 'I tell you the truth, no one can see the kingdom of God unless he is born again. Flesh gives

birth to flesh, but the Spirit gives birth to spirit.' " *(John 3:3, 6).*

"As for you, the anointing you received from him remains in you, and you do not need anyone to teach you." (1 John 2:27)

Praying It In

O Lord,
how often
I have tried
to explain Your Word
to "deaf" people!
Why could I not
understand
that without ears to hear
they could not
possibly respond?
Thank You for
unsealing my ears,
for opening my eyes,
and for delivering me
from Satan's kingdom
to enjoy
a whole new world
I never knew existed.
Will You open
the eyes of others today
that they too may see You?
Amen.

SEARCHING THE BIBLE FOR MYSELF

58

*STEP SIX: "If you look for it as for silver and search
for it as for hidden treasure." (2:4)*

We now come to our last two steps in search of God's wisdom. Just because I have called on God for understanding, I cannot sit back and expect Him to zap me, hoping that, when I come to, I will be fully loaded with His wisdom. It simply does not work that way. Whereas I must pray as if it all depends on God, I must also search as if it all depends on me. I play my part; then God, as if by coincidence, graciously gives me wisdom (2:6).

Job 28 is a thrilling account of a treasure hunt. With an intended link, the question is asked there "Where can wisdom be found?" The juxtapositioning of these two topics joins God's grace in giving with my labor of searching.

As I come to the Bible, I call out for insight. I get down to the hard work of reading, meditating, musing and pondering. I pray until the light penetrates my mind and settles in my spirit. The novice may give up easily without struggling with the text. Those who persevere are richly rewarded. God the Holy Spirit shows us the meaning of the Word He originally inspired. Who better could we ask for insight than the overseer of men's pens as they "were carried along by the Holy Spirit" (2 Peter 1:21)?

However, I have discovered the most important truths lie "near the surface." Mining them is not painstaking. While hungry, studious types enjoy digging out those treasures deeper in the mine shaft, God shows His fairness in giving everyone, studious or not, equal opportunity to understand the essentials.

Despite my large library, I find the times of greatest revelation come when I have only a Bible or Testament. At an airport or in some line-up, God surprises me. He breaks into my dimness by flashing amazing light on the sacred page.

The joy of discovery that comes to those who persevere is something you'll not want to miss. Some seekers develop such an insatiable thirst for truth they forget even to eat. On more than one occasion I have held up my hand, saying, "Stop, Lord, I can't take any more—I've got spiritual indigestion!"

Of course, there are times when, as a teacher, I need to dig deeper in the shaft, using my study aids. Sometimes, after pursuing a thought, I notice eight or ten open volumes cluttering my desk. Gradually it dawns what has happened. Finding I needed help understanding, I had pulled down two or three translations. Then an encyclopedia. Then an atlas. Then a lexicon or commentary. In the middle of this process, being gloriously lost in truth-revealing research, the telephone may ring. I spend a half hour counseling a needy person.

Putting the phone down, I notice the pile. *What in the world was I doing with all these books?* I wonder. Rabbit trail led to rabbit trail, until forgetting my original purpose, I became drenched with the joy of discovery. Like a scientist in his lab, I discovered the fascinating answers to questions I had never thought of asking. Humbly, in thanksgiving, I would kneel at my "serendipity chair."

The chair was an inexpensive leatherette armchair. For years it graced my study. Every time God gave me a flash of insight from Scripture I would kneel there in front of it to give thanks to the great Revealer. But just in case I thought the revelation came to me as a reward for my imagined super-spirituality, God had a way of cutting me down to size. As I prayed, my kneecap would stick into an eight or nine inch horizontal slit in the lower front of the chair.

I'm ashamed to confess that some years before—not as many as I would like to think—I had kicked the chair in a fleshly outburst of anger (now repented of but never far from my mind). As I prayed, it was as if God was saying, "Don't let those insights swell your head. You're the one who kicked that chair and you'd better remember that when you preach!"

Somewhat sobering? I'll say so!

Thinking It Through

Before you read the Word today, give thanks to God for (a) the ability to read—something denied many in the world; (b) a mind with which to think and understand; and (c) the dedication and sacrifice of those, often burned at the stake, who risked their lives by translating the Bible into your language. May you treasure these gifts and use them to the full.

Planting It Deep

"The commands of the LORD are radiant, giving light to the eyes. . . . They are more precious than gold, than

much pure gold; they are sweeter than honey, than honey from the comb." (Psalm 19:8, 10).

Praying It In

O Lord,
how could I have gone
all those years
without realizing
there were so many joys
waiting to be discovered?
Because You touched me,
my soul is consumed with longing
for Your Word.
As I read and study it,
I want You to know
that I completely depend
on You
for deeper insight,
and for the desire
to practice
what I find there.
Amen.

FINDING THE RIGHT WAY TO LIVE

59

*STEP SEVEN: "Then you will understand the fear
of the LORD and find the knowledge of God." (2:5)*

At last we reach the goal! God had said, "You will seek
me and find me when you seek me with all your heart"
(Jeremiah 29:13). We have accepted, stored, turned, applied,
called and searched. Now we are rewarded. "Then," says
Proverbs 2:5, "you will understand the fear of the Lord and
find the knowledge of God."

But no sooner do we get to this mountaintop of finding,
than we see above us another whole mountain range, still un-
conquered. We come to realize that our finding brought us
only to the first base camp. There are many more to go as we
keep climbing. The search for God's wisdom is an ongoing
journey. Our task, this side of heaven, is never complete.
We've not arrived until we see Him who is the personification
of all true wisdom.

Maybe the way I now look at things will change, but I find
myself hoping that even then, the joy of discovering His wisdom and ways will never end. I sense that there will be so
much more than we ever imagined that it will take eternity to
explore! "Oh, the depth of the riches of the wisdom and
knowledge of God!" says Paul in Romans 11:33, 36, "How

unsearchable his judgments and his paths beyond tracing out. . . . To Him be the glory forever! Amen."

Derek Kidner, in his fine commentary on Proverbs, sees two expressions in our verse which he calls "the poles of awe and intimacy." "The fear of the LORD" and "the knowledge of God" are, he tells us, "the two classic Old Testament terms for true religion."[1] If then you have sought wisdom with a spirit of reverence and humility, it should produce these very results in your life.

First, it will form in you a deeper awareness of the holiness, majesty and splendor of our God. This will result in your being immersed in a sense of awe and wonder (the fear of the Lord), forcing you figuratively to take your shoes from off your feet as you realize that the place on which you stand is holy ground.

Second, it will enrich the closeness of your relationship with this great God. For "the knowledge of God," as used here, is not mere cerebral inflammation but rather an actual relationship which is of a personal and experiential nature. Although the root from which "knowledge" is derived has many meanings, it is still the intimate word used in the classic euphemism "And Adam knew his wife, and she conceived and bare Cain" (Genesis 4:1, KJV).

This balance, then, of awe and intimacy should characterize my relationship with this God of all wisdom. The snug closeness of my having "stilled and quieted my soul; like a weaned child with its mother" (Psalm 131:2) will not produce such unrestrained liberty that I forget the greatness and holiness of this One whose presence should produce in me a deep and reverential awe.

While we have gone through the seven steps needed to find true wisdom, we must not just leave it there as if there were no other purpose than self-fulfillment and the joy of discovery. We must remind ourselves yet again that the purpose of thirsting after God is not so we can become seclusive mystics enjoying those subjective feelings running up and down our spines. Rather it is that we will be able to live lives of holiness and usefulness.

The rest of Proverbs chapter 2 puts our thirst for wisdom into that proper biblical context. *Verses 9-11* teach that those who live by God's standards find that this Life with a capital L is thoroughly enjoyable as we put His wisdom into practice. *Verses 12-19* note that such wisdom can be expected to provide protection both from wicked men and seductive women. *Verses 20-22*, the final paragraph, show that the nature of true wisdom is to guide us in following the right people and walking in the right paths.

Thus the pleasant paths of Christian living all begin with thirsting after God's wisdom as described in our six verses. May His Spirit produce such a longing in us!

Thinking It Through

Sit down and ponder: Which of the two results of thirsting after God's wisdom has been most evident in your life? The comforting sense of feeling close and snug in your relationship with God? Or your increasing grasp of the greatness and holiness of this great God? Be honest and recognize which one of those two now needs more cultivating. Then ask God to develop that balance in your life.

Planting It Deep

"Be strong and very courageous. Be careful to obey all the law my servant Moses gave you; do not turn from it to the right or to the left, that you may be successful wherever you go." (Joshua 1:7)

Praying It In

O Lord,
I used to be
fearful of Your holiness
because I had
no relationship with You.
Now You have brought me
into Your great family,
help me not to be
so taken up with
"sitting on Your lap"
that I forget
You are still
the great and holy One
who inhabits eternity
and that none
could ever approach You
except through
Jesus Christ.
To You be all the glory.
Amen.

A Prayer

Lord,
forgive me for thinking
I could be wise is my own wisdom.
It has proved inadequate—
in fact, useless—
time and time again.

Thank you for giving us the Bible,
the most precious book this world affords.
I have thought about what it cost
to get it to us
in our own language.
I thank you for the men and women
who were willing to die
so I could be told about you,
for those hundreds burned at the stake
so I could have a copy.

As I open it for instruction day by day,
grant me a meek and submissive spirit
that Your wisdom may have great impact
upon my life.
Amen.

PART SEVEN

Finding

Matthew 5:1-10

¹Now when he saw the crowds, he went up on a mountainside and sat down. His disciples came to him, ²and he began to teach them, saying:

³"Blessed are the poor in spirit,
    for theirs is the kingdom of heaven.
⁴Blessed are those who mourn,
    for they will be comforted.
⁵Blessed are the meek,
    for they will inherit the earth.
⁶Blessed are those who hunger and thirst
        for righteousness,
    for they will be filled.
⁷Blessed are the merciful,
    for they will be shown mercy.
⁸Blessed are the pure in heart,
    for they will see God.
⁹Blessed are the peacemakers,
    for they will be called sons of God.
¹⁰Blessed are those who are persecuted
        because of righteousness,
    for theirs is the kingdom of heaven."

THE LONGING TO BE CHANGED

60

"Blessed are those who hunger and thirst for righteousness, for they will be filled." (Matthew 5:6)

Just as in our last segment, the true searcher finds wisdom, so it is with God Himself—those who truly seek Him will find.

I shall never forget the light dawning when, as a young man, I first read those two superb volumes on The Sermon on the Mount by fellow Welshman Martyn Lloyd-Jones. They helped me answer many lingering questions: Why are thirsty people blessed? How can they be filled? Can they lose that filling? Jones helped me see that the sevenfold description of the Christian character in Matthew 5:3-9 is in fact also the pathway to becoming a true Christian.

These beatitudes (or states of blessedness) have been called "the mountain" in the sermon. The first three (5:3-5) lead us up to the point of meeting God and longing for Him. The fourth (5:6) is the peak. Then the last three (5:7-9) show us coming from the mountain to live as changed people among our fellow humans.

You will soon notice these seven statements are the virtual antithesis of what man's wisdom teaches. They are really paradoxes or apparent contradictions. There are many such concepts in the New Testament, because the kingdom of God is an upside-down (really an upside-up) kingdom. It opposes worldly standards.

But let me enlarge on this.

The first three beatitudes (5:3-5) are the way we come to God for salvation; poverty of spirit (5:3) leading to mourning over sin (5:4) producing a teachable spirit (5:5). Only this route brings us to *the fourth beatitude*—hunger and thirst for God's ways (5:6). We see we can never, of ourselves, please God, and we become desperate to find His remedy. The filling of verse 6 is God's gracious response to our longing.

The last three beatitudes (5:7-9) are evidence that God lives in us, forming the character of Christ. Christians become merciful, pure in heart and peacemakers.

The "blessed" in each verse is a richer dimension than the world's "happiness." It is like the Jewish *shalom*—total well-being. Each beatitude is one ingredient of the recipe. All seven refer to the same person.

But these seven qualities also describe our ongoing lifestyle. We continue to pursue them all our lives. Joining the *first* line of each verse provides a description of the Christian life. Compare them with the sevenfold fruit of the Spirit (Galatians 5: 22-23). Joining the *last* lines of all seven lets us see where this leads.

The eighth (different) beatitude, persecution (Matthew 5:10) is not sought, but will likely come as a result of living righteously.

In our next segment we shall see what it means to hunger and thirst, but look for a moment at this central verse 6 as a whole. It tells us three things:

a) The longing is for righteousness.

b) The condition is hungering and thirsting.

c) The promise is blessing and satisfaction.

We shall scratch the surface of just the first here.

1. *The longing is for righteousness*—"Blessed are those who hunger and thirst after righteousness." Happiness is never the goal, but always the by-product of righteousness. En route, God is more interested in our holiness than our happiness. The path will have obstacles. But the resulting "blessedness" more than makes up for them.

The righteousness mentioned is the longing to be free from sinful thoughts and deeds, from both the power and the very desire for sin. It includes personal and societal righteousness. A changed person then becomes light and salt, righteously influencing a darkened and corrupt society.

It embraces three types of righteousness. *First,* the righteousness God freely imputes because of Jesus' death; *second,* the actual reproduction of Christ's life in me (i.e., the fruit of the Spirit); *third,* the contagious spreading of this righteousness, potentially influencing a nation.

Any other "quick-fix" method to change a people will prove manufactured, short-lived and easily reversible.

Thinking It Through

Sorrow for sin is not popular today. Yet the Bible balances the "goodness and severity" of God. A century ago we emphasized God's severity; today we prefer to speak of God's goodness (for we dislike anything that smells negative). I need to ask myself, *Did I really go through this sorrow for sin? Do I still? Do I long for righteousness all around and within?* If not, I know of no other route to thirsting after God. But if such sorrow does grip me, I will need no persuasion to hunger and thirst.

Planting It Deep

"For I know my transgressions, and my sin is always before me. Against you, you only, have I sinned and done what is evil in your sight. . . . Create in me a pure heart, O God. . . . Restore to me the joy of your salvation." (Psalm 51:3-4, 10, 12)

Praying It In

O Lord,
I must admit:
it seems I came to You
on my terms.
I thought I had faith, Lord,
but I did not have
any sense of guilt
about my sin.
I want now
to honestly face that.
Then,
seeing my great need
will surely make me turn
to love You more and more.
Show me again
Your great mercy!
Amen.

THE CONDITION AND THE PROMISE

61

*"Blessed are those who hunger and thirst for righteousness,
for they will be filled." (Matthew 5:6)*

Having seen in our last segment that the longing is for righteousness, we now see:

2. *The condition is hungering and thirsting.* Hungering and thirsting after righteousness is to hunger and thirst after God. And it gradually reaches a point of desperation. "Their tongues are parched with thirst" (Isaiah 41:17).

We saw that filling our inner vacuum with substitutes can smother our thirst. Only when we "accept no substitutes" do we become conscious of our emptiness and cry out for God. We shall see that if we are genuine, we will never be "satisfied" for long. The more we have the more we'll want!

Lloyd-Jones suggests five ways to test whether we are hungry. They are

1. Do I see through my own false righteousness?
2. Do I avoid everything that opposes righteousness?
3. Do I avoid what takes the edge off my spiritual appetite?
4. Do I keep reminding myself what righteousness actually is?
5. Do I grasp every opportunity to pursue it?

"But," you say, "Look at my schedule! Where have I time to actively pursue it?" Ah! "If you are hungering and thirsting you'll *find* time," says Jones. "You will order your life; you will say, 'First things must come first; there is a priority in these matters and I cannot afford to neglect this because my soul is in bondage.' "[1] It is amazing how we find time to do what we want to do. Those who hunger and thirst after righteousness do not merely want—they are frantic!

3. *The promise is blessedness and satisfaction.* "They will be filled." What a glorious promise this is. Those with a sense of hopelessness and defeat will be given what they long for. God has done all He needs to, so we can find fulness of life. The ball is now in our court. We must meet the condition—hungering and thirsting—and the promise will be ours, all because of God's grace.

If you are lacking spiritual hunger, just eat without it! For it is in eating and drinking (even without sensing need) that you become hungry and thirsty. "But," you say, "the filling of this verse is dependent on my hungering and thirsting. Even if I get that, then once I am filled, it will end. For, no thirst, no blessing!"

You do not refuse food because you ate a week ago, nor does the temporary satisfaction from one drink last for long. So it is spiritually. But (and here's the big difference) when it comes to the spiritual, the drink itself will actually intensify your thirst, bringing not lasting satisfaction but greater longing.

Once we "taste and see that the Lord is good," we become hooked. We shall keep wanting more. The promise you will "never thirst again" (see John 4:14) does not mean you will never want more, but that you'll have the supply within you.

You are an empty thimble. You hunger and thirst for God. God dips you into the ocean of His love. You come up full. But no sooner do you pronounce the final "d" of "satisfied" than God changes you into a bucket. So again you cry to be filled. He graciously grants your longing, but with that filling, changes you into a barrel. With each filling, you receive an increased capacity. In this way you are both filled and thirsty at the same time.

Perhaps one day I will be fully filled. And yet, I secretly hope the hymn which says, "Bread of heaven, feed me till I want no more," is as wrong when it refers to heaven as it is here on earth. Even in eternity I hope I will go on discovering fresh things every day. We shall have to wait and see!

Thinking It Through

If you're not thirsty, only drinking will bring it about. When you don't feel like reading the Word, read it anyway. When you don't feel like praising God, praise Him anyway. When you are not inclined to thanksgiving, thank Him anyway. When you are not inclined to pray—keep on praying. For it is in the doing that you get the longing. And that longing will soon turn to desperation!

Planting It Deep

"The poor and needy search for water, but there is none; their tongues are parched with thirst. . . . I will make rivers flow on barren heights, and springs within the valleys. I will turn the desert into pools of water, and the parched ground into springs." (Isaiah 41:17-18)

Praying It In

O Lord,
I am so used
to doing
what I feel like doing,
that it's hard to eat
when I'm not hungry!
Give me a sense
of the need
to lay down
spiritual absolutes,
like
"When I don't feel thirsty,
I will drink anyway"
Then I will be confident
I can leave the rest
to You!
Amen.

Epilogue

TEN SUGGESTIONS ON HOW A CHRISTIAN CAN CULTIVATE A DEEPER THIRST AFTER GOD

1. Keep Track

Keep track for a whole week of the people, possessions, topics and pleasures (other than God) which occupy most of your thinking or bring you the greatest enjoyment in life (e.g. friends, family members, car, sports, television, business matters, music, church functions, hobbies, sleeping, etc). This is best done by taking a few minutes to record your observations before retiring each night. You may produce a more objective list by showing your draft to the person who spends most time with you each week. He or she may be more honest!

2. Assign

Assign (as first, second and third) the three items on your list which would be hardest to give up.

3. Read

Read Mark 15:16-20 thoughtfully and prayerfully, meditating on this fact: "Jesus went through all this because of His love and commitment to me."

4. Ponder

Thoughtfully ponder Philippians 2:5-11. List on paper what Jesus was willing to give up and go through for you. After thinking about God's purpose found in verses 10-11, seriously ponder what it would mean for you to give up such valued relationships, possessions, positions or pleasures in your life.

5. Kneel

When you are ready, kneel in quietness and invite Jesus Christ to become the Lord and Master of every aspect of your life. Then, with your list of priorities before you, prayerfully add "Jesus Christ is Lord" and assign to this entry the number one position on your list.

6. Reassign

Now reconsider your previous first, second and third items. Provided they are compatible with Christianity (i.e., helping, not hindering, your growth), reassign them to numbers 2, 3 and 4 positions respectively. If they are not compatible or are a hindrance, ask God to give you the courage to strike them off your list altogether

7. Allocate

Allocate a twenty-minute period daily (preferably early morning) to meet with God and think about Him and His kingdom. Plan carefully before deciding when and where you will do this as it will likely mean sacrificing something the night before or early that morning.

8. Meditate

Carefully guard this time slot to read and meditate on a short portion of the Bible daily (there are many fine quiet time aids or daily reading booklets available at any Christian bookstore). In prayer, talk to God about what you learn. Persevere, especially on the days when—like me—you may not seem to find as much, for there will be those. Choose one thought from the passage and ask God to help you to apply that principle to *all* you do that day. Christians should have no double standards.

9. Contemplate

Now move beyond meditating on the Word to contemplating God the Author. Ability in this will take some practice and perseverance. Keep at it—it will gradually come. And do not be satisfied when you begin to enjoy it. You must keep on until you are addicted not only to the Bible (good though that is) but to God Himself. Seek Him "beyond the sacred page." You can judge your progress as you notice other items on your list becoming less and less important. Don't forget: it is the good that is often the enemy of the best.

10. Determine

Determine not to be a private Christian. Look for ways to influence and bless others by your new lifestyle. Private worship should prepare you to contribute by your presence to the public worship of the church, God's primary institution. Then you will be better equipped to start serving others through your church.

Thinking It Through

1. What have you learned as you read through this book? Would three important lessons come to mind?

2. As you read the book, what unresolved matters from your past came into your mind? What are you now willing to do about them?

3. Is there a course of action to which you would now be willing to commit yourself? Is there someone close to you with whom you could share this and ask to pray with you?

Planting It Deep

"The sluggard craves and gets nothing, but the desires of the diligent are fully satisfied." (Proverbs 13:4)

Praying It In

O Lord,
I guess this is the crunch!
If I'm not moved
to do something
about my life
now,
I'll likely
put it off indefinitely!
Move me to action, Lord—
wise action,
which will prove valuable
a year from now.
Give me a new commitment
with discipline
and diligence, Lord.
Because I really am thirsty,
and I do know
You are the Answer.
Amen.

A Prayer

by my mentor, A.W. Tozer

O Lord,
I have heard a good word
inviting me to
look away to Thee
and be satisfied.

My heart longs to respond,
but sin has clouded my vision
till I see Thee but dimly.

Be pleased to cleanse me
in Thine own precious blood,
and make me inwardly pure,
so that I may with unveiled eyes
gaze upon Thee
all the days
of my earthly pilgrimage.

Then shall I be prepared
to behold Thee in full splendour
in the day
when Thou shalt appear
to be glorified
in Thy saints
and admired
in all them that believe.
Amen.[1]

Rabbit Trails for Digging Deeper

RABBIT TRAIL # 1

MORE ABOUT SEEING GOD'S GLORY

(to follow segment 26, pages 124-127)

Now that you have read segment 26, you may want to think more about how God shows Himself to sinful man. This rabbit trail will prepare us to better understand the next few segments in our journey towards reflecting the glory of God (as Moses did in Exodus 34:29).

Moses pleads, "Show me your glory." God's glory is His 'radiant splendor' (literally 'the weight' of God). It is everything I can know about this glorious God.

God answers Moses by saying, "I will make all my 'goodness' pass in front of you" (Exodus 33:19). The word "goodness" here has great breadth to it. It speaks of God's nature, the essence of his glory. When God declares here His heart of mercy and compassion, He is giving Moses an addictive glimpse into His character. God also says, "I will proclaim my name." And He does just that in 34:6. "The name of God" is another way of referring to God's nature or character and is often used this way in the Bible. It even covers the way we are to live our lives (as in Micah 4:5).

In His covenant relationship with the people of Israel, God's revealed name was "YHWH" (various spellings include JHVH, IHVH, JHWH). We call this the Tetragrammaton (four letters). We usually pronounce it "Yahweh" when the vowels are provided, or less correctly, but much-loved because of our many hymns, "Jehovah." It is printed in capitals as LORD in most English Bibles.

Scholars tell us that Yahweh is a form of the verb "to be," perhaps a condensing of "I am that I am" as God revealed Himself to Moses in Exodus 3:14. It likely means "He is," or "He who continually is." (I like to describe Him as the God-of-the-ever-present-tense.) Beyond this they find it difficult to penetrate with certainty the fathomlessness of that name. As with God's name, so with God's nature. Finite beings can never fully grasp the hidden depths. Only the infinite can comprehend the infinite.

Even what we do know about God's nature must be revealed by Him. Such self-disclosure appears to be progressive in Scripture (dreams, visions, theophanies, etc.). But the fullest and most illuminating is in the person of Jesus Christ Himself. For He is God incarnate ("in flesh"). The New Testament says, "In these last days he has spoken to us by [in] his Son . . . the radiance of God's glory and the exact representation of His being" (Hebrews 1:2-3).

Jacob's "face-to-face" experience at Jabbok (see Genesis 32 and Hosea 12:2-4) was one of seeing God in human form, perhaps the more usual type of theophany (appearance of God) in the Bible. Such incidents in Scripture likely show us an activity of the Christ, the second person of the Trinity, prior to His New Testament incarnation. It seems too that He is almost always the One referred to when the phrase "the angel of the LORD" occurs, as with Moses at the burning bush. (Compare Exodus 3:2 with 3:4.)

But even then, while on earth, God the Son was still veiled by a human body. The essence of His unveiled glory would doubtless have been too much for us sinful creatures to gaze on. Despite this, in His gracious appetite-whetting way, God made it possible for that glory to fleetingly break through (see Luke 9:28-36; John 1:14).

When it came to communion with the Living God, nobody in the Old Testament was more privileged than Moses. He saw more of God than anyone on earth, though still not as much as those can see who are in heaven.

God spoke of His "hand" and His "back" (anthropomorphisms, descriptions in human terms, used for our benefit, to describe this God who is non-corporeal Spirit). God conveys to Moses that although he would see more of God than he had before, there would still be a limit—not in what God was able to reveal, but in what Moses could bear.

God's "back" may be a figurative way of saying the "after-effects" of God's presence. But God says in Exodus 33:20, "you cannot see my face, for no one may see me and live." Moses' revelation then, though extra special, would still be partial. How wonderful that in the last chapter of the Bible, God says of His servants, "they shall see His face." This expression is meant to convey a closer encounter again than that of Moses' speaking with God "face-to-face" (33:11).

Just to think that all those whose trust is in Christ alone will have this inestimable privilege! What a glorious prospect! How needful that we prepare ourselves for that great sight by taking advantage, through regular quiet times, of what God is wanting us to know of Him now. As we ponder and become increasingly aware of God's holiness, Thomas Binney's great hymn captures our predicament so well:

> Eternal Light! Eternal Light!
>   How pure the soul must be
> When placed within Thy searching sight,
> It shrinks not, but with calm delight
>   Can live, and look on Thee!

The spirits that surround Thy throne
　　May bear the burning bliss;
But that is surely theirs alone,
Since they have never, never known
　　A fallen world like this.

Oh, how shall I, whose native sphere
　　Is dark, whose mind is dim,
Before the Ineffable appear,
And on my naked spirit bear
　　The uncreated beam?

There is a way for man to rise
　　To that sublime abode;
An offering and a sacrifice,
A Holy Spirit's energies.
　　An Advocate with God:

These, these prepare us for the sight
　　Of holiness above;
The sons of ignorance and night
May dwell in the Eternal Light,
　　Thro' the Eternal Love.[1]

298 THIRSTING AFTER GOD

RABBIT TRAIL # 2

ANOTHER KIND OF GLORY

(to follow segment 38, pages 178-181)

NOTE: If you are a new Christian, this rabbit trail will stretch your mind. But do your best to persevere in understanding it. It isn't long. Even reading it through will help you grasp something of the greatness of God's plan to bring salvation. It will also help in showing you the direction to turn to see the glory of God.

There is a different kind of way altogether by which God was pleased to show us His glory. This outstanding self-disclosure of God is in the Person of Jesus Christ. "For God, who said, 'let light shine out of darkness,' made His light shine in our hearts to give us the light of the knowledge of the glory of God in the face of Christ" (2 Corinthians 4:6).

The writer to the Hebrews says, "In the past God spoke to our forefathers through the prophets, at many times and in various ways, but in these last days he has spoken to us by his Son, whom he appointed heir of all things and through whom he made the universe" (Hebrews 1:1-2). This was no mere reflection. This was God in human form! For "the Son is the radiance of God's glory and the exact representation of his being" (1:3). The disciples walked with One who was actually God!

Yet, so that He could be seen (for God is Spirit), He was made flesh. But that body is also called a veil. A veil in Scripture is meant to conceal. And indeed, Jesus' body had both a revealing and a concealing purpose. Notice now the two main 'veils' in the Bible:

1. The Veil of the Temple. God gave the emancipated Israelites a detailed plan for constructing the meeting place (a tent) for the long desert journey. The Bible calls this the Tabernacle, (related to our English word "tavern," a temporary dwelling-place or inn). This interim structure later became the more ornate Temple.

God decreed that a veil, or curtain, was to hang between the two inner rooms. These were (a) the Holy Place, where the priests served daily, and (b) the Most Holy Place, or Holy of Holies, entered only by the High Priest once a year. The curtain separated these two rooms. Concealed behind that curtain in the inner room—the Most Holy Place—was a special box called the ark of the testimony, over which God's glory would be seen (Exodus 25:22). The curtain was to veil or conceal that glory.

2. The Body of Jesus Christ. Because Jesus is, always was and always will be God Himself ("the exact representation of [God's] being" [Hebrews 1:3]), such glory had to be veiled, so man could look on Him. This was done by His being clothed with a human body at the incarnation. John expresses it beautifully in his gospel: "The Word became flesh and made His dwelling [literally "tabernacled" or "pitched His tent"] among us. We have seen his glory, the glory of the One and Only, who came from the Father, full of grace and truth" (1:14). Though He was God, the disciples could look upon Him because that divine glory was shrouded by His body.

How meaningful it is, therefore, that these two main biblical references to a veil, the Tabernacle and Christ's body, are compared and contrasted in the New Testament. The Old Testament veil (in the tabernacle) is considered the shadow, while the New Testament Veil (the Body of Jesus) is shown to be the substance. Both were meeting places where God would conceal, but later reveal His glory. Jesus' body would gloriously replace the Temple veil.

As Jesus was crucified on the cross, bearing God's punishment on our sin, He breathed His last breath at the ninth hour of the day (3 p.m.). At that hour, the on-duty priest was offering the evening sacrifice in the Holy Place. He would be standing at most a few feet from the altar of incense, likely facing the Veil. (For these details read Exodus 30:1-8; Luke 1:8-10; Acts 3:1).

At that precise moment, as if by some great Damocles' sword, the Veil of the Temple "was torn in two from top to bottom" (Matthew 27:51), thus giving unhindered view and access into the very place where God's presence and glory had been specially manifested.

One can imagine the holy horror with which that priest must have fled from the room. (Such a vision under Old Testament rules spelled death.) Is this why "a large number of priests became obedient to the faith" (Acts 6:7)? Did the cloud of incense from that altar effectively conceal the Shekinah Glory, so he would not die? I think not!

God opened the curtain for the same reason He rolled away the stone from Jesus' tomb three days later; it was to reveal its emptiness, and show that His glory was no longer in the temple building, but in the person of Jesus. A temple veil was no longer necessary, for the glory had departed!

But the veil of Christ's body was also "torn" in crucifixion. Whereas this enabled us to see some of His glory (John 17:1), Hebrews explains that because of Jesus' death, "we have confidence to enter the Most Holy Place by the blood of Jesus, by a new and living way opened for us *through the curtain, that is, His body"* (Hebrews 10:19-20, emphasis added).

The purpose of the old curtain or veil was now finished. A new veil, Jesus' body (which had shrouded His glory), had taken its place. It is now through Jesus, not through temple ritual, that we come into God's presence, without fear.

That is why we pray "in the name (through the Person) of Jesus." The old veil barred entry, the new veil welcomes.

If you have struggled through this, congratulations. Truth is grasped gradually, not suddenly.

RABBIT TRAIL # 3

DETERMINING JUST WHERE I STAND

(to follow segment 46, pages 216-219)

This rabbit trail is intended to lay a foundation for under-standing how to present my body as a living sacrifice. We shall start with what takes place when a person is first presented with the claims of the gospel. We will then build on that.

As the Good News of the cross is presented to unbelievers, the Holy Spirit seeks to convict them of sin. This amazing truth may, sooner or later, dawn on them and start to make sense. They have reached a crossroads! They can go in one of four possible directions.

Direction Number One

Some will halt their investigations at this crossroads. The cost of discipleship begins to sink in. Wanting to retain con-trol, they go no further. But unless they smother their thoughts, an offending conscience will continually blotch their lives. They live unhappily between two worlds.

Direction Number Two

Without realizing the need for a radical change, some will profess a simple faith in Christ. But while they have "accepted Him as Savior," nobody has explained to them that the first word of the gospel is repentance, essential if they are to become transformed people. This volitional change is not just remorse (emotional response) nor regret (intellectual response). It is meant to be a response of the mind, emotions and will.

Nevertheless, I believe that God still accepts the sincerity of that first step of faith. He always meets us where we are! But if genuine it will not be long before these people get more "light" and are faced with the need to repent. Until they do that, they remain king of their own castle, crown intact.

Direction Number Three

There are those who do see the need for repentance but who stop short of yielding their will. Their "decision for Christ" appears to be genuine, but they choose to ignore, put off or forget about repentance. This parody of faith is little more than superficial. The person believes only cerebrally. Because God holds us accountable for the light we have received, this person ignores the repentance element to their peril!

We cannot pick and choose which of God's requirements we will meet, looking upon the rest as mere optional extras, to be pursued at some later, more convenient time.

A decision without repentance is a caricature of Christian conversion, devoid of biblical reality. Tozer spoke out against such a diluted religion: "Faith," he said, "may now be exercised without a jar to the moral life and without embarrassment to the Adamic ego. Christ may be 'received' without creating any special love for Him in the soul of the receiver. The man is 'saved' but he is not hungry or thirsty after God."[1]

Such teaching bears little resemblance to God's Word. Let it be shouted from the rooftops that this is not what the Bible means by Christian conversion. Such nominal evangelicalism is more hazardous than the nominal Christianity which evangelicals repudiate. To think smugly that having "the truth" in words will bring the same result as experiencing the reality of a changed life is the not-so-thin end of a very dangerous wedge.

Direction Number Four

This group becomes truly Christian. A deep sense of sinfulness drives them to the cross of Christ. In genuine repentance they plead for forgiveness, wanting to follow Jesus for the rest of their lives. They have responded to all they know God wants of them. They will doubtless keep on grasping more and more of what it means to follow.

Mind, emotions and will have responded to His convicting grace. God has pulled up the blinds which had kept the human spirit in the dark. He has let in the sunshine of His life and love, by regenerating them. This was brought about only by the Holy Spirit, who, as God, then takes up residence within that human spirit. The person is born anew and part of God's family.

At this point our main track (Segment 46) and this rabbit trail actually converge.

A few who, through repentance come to faith in Christ, also at that same time present their bodies as living sacrifices. In a totality of surrender, they give God all they are and have from that very first step of faith. Indeed, I see no biblical reason why this should not be the norm. Perhaps our preaching is not clear or convicting enough!

However, most of us reach this point of full commitment some time after conversion. Otherwise, why would the apostle be urging these Christians to take this next step? (Romans 12:1)

Before such surrender, a Christian deprives the Holy Spirit of His right to enter secret rooms in his life. The Spirit is restricted to that person's human spirit. This is analogous to locking a "lodger" in his rented room only to discover that he is actually the owner of the whole house!

Because the Bible tells me (1 Thessalonians 5:23) I am spirit and soul and body, God now wants access to each part. Then all areas of my personal, family, business and community life will be controlled by these principles.

Have I then presented my body to God? If sincere, I should be able to replace the word "body" in our Romans 12 text with any of its individual parts. Have I presented my eyes so that I am conscious of what I look at? Have I presented my tongue so I will be careful not to offend? Have I presented my right foot so that when I drive I observe the speed limit and obey "every ordinance of man for the Lord's sake"?

In this way the Holy Spirit will not merely reside in me but fill me. For "present your bodies" is merely another way of saying "be filled with the Spirit"!

RABBIT TRAIL # 4

BLUE MONDAY

by Rosemary Price

(to follow segment 28, pages 132-135)

It was one of those blue Monday mornings. I could feel it in my bones as I crawled out of bed, stretching and yawning, and made my way to the bathroom. A late night, a succession of visitors and a hectic weekend were now taking their toll.

Tousled hair and a tired face greeted me in the mirror. Ugh! Outside, heavy rain drummed on the roof and dripped rhythmically through a leaking roof gutter.

I made my way downstairs to clean up the debris from Sunday evening and to start breakfast for the family. But Suki, the cat, was determined to eat first. She rubbed against my legs and meowed constantly until I gave in and opened her "gourmet" breakfast.

What a pest, I thought. *Why can't those lazy kids feed their silly cat themselves? Now I smell of cat food, and I'll have to wash my hands again.*

Still grumbling to myself, I put the bread in the toaster and waited. Nothing. Someone had plugged in the iron on the other counter, and now the fuse was blown. Meanwhile, a burnt smell from the stove announced that the porridge was ready.

"Mum, have you seen my gray skirt?" shouted my younger daughter.

My mild, "No, dear," masked the unkind thoughts churning in my mind. *Why doesn't she hang up her clothes? Why are my kids so messy?*

At that moment, my son's trumpet-like bellow rushed down the stairs, competing with the radio music in his sister's bedroom. "Mum, are my sandwiches ready? I've got to go in ten minutes! I can't find any socks!"

A more mature voice, in kinder tones, called from another direction. "Did you remember to iron my shirt, dear? I've got an important appointment and have to leave soon."

Checking the impulse to tell everyone to look after themselves for a change, I assumed the air of a martyr. With a new fuse installed, I started to iron the shirt, while at the same time admonishing anyone approaching the toaster to wait until I'd finished.

At last the family was fed, sandwiches made, hurried good-byes said, and the front door finally closed. My quick glance took in the chaos of the kitchen: the sink full of dishes, the jam-streaked tablecloth with its centerpiece askew, and the morning newspaper lying open on the floor.

I bent to pick up the paper, and a line caught my eye. It was about somebody vacationing in the Bahamas. Visions of golden sand, swaying palm trees and crystal blue water passed through my mind. I imagined mouth-watering meals served on shady patios by courteous, smiling waiters, bowing politely to my every whim. Tears of self-pity welled up in my tired eyes. *I'm the one who should be on holiday in the sun. I deserve a break.* Dabbing my tears away, I started to tackle the dishes.

With some semblance of order restored to the kitchen, and before trudging upstairs to face the bedrooms, I sat down with my Bible. I was reading consecutively through the gospels.

Suddenly, the words "Jesus felt compassion for her" leapt out at me. Elsewhere, I read that He had compassion for the multitudes.

But me, Lord? I asked. *I'm just a tired, disgruntled homemaker with a messy home and too little time. I'm not sick or hungry or poor.* But I read on—and as the minutes elapsed, I just knew *He cared,* for each person and problem. Everybody matters to Him!

Strangely, my self-pity evaporated and thankfulness filled my heart. Thankfulness for the Lord Jesus who had done so much for me. Thankfulness for my family, and even for my messy house.

As I sat there, a ray of sunshine actually broke though the clouds, flooding the room with beauty and light. *It's going to be a lovely day!* I realized. Humming under my breath, and with renewed strength, I hurried upstairs to get on with the rest of this promising day.

Used by permission of Interest *magazine. Originally written several years ago when the children were younger. Rosemary is the wife of Keith Price.*

NOTES

Chapter 4

1 B.F. (arr.), "O Christ, in Thee My Soul Hath Found," *Keswick Hymn-book* (Toronto: Marshall, Morgan and Scott: n.d.), # 425.

Part Two

1 Abraham Joshua Heschel, "I Asked for Wonder," edited by Samuel H. Dresner (Crossroad, NY: n.p., 1998), p. 10.

Chapter 8

1 Gerhard Tersteegen, *Sermons and Hymns*, vol. 2, trans. John Wesley (Hampton, TN: Harvey & Tait, 1976, repr. 1998).

Chapter 9

1 Austin Miles, "In the Garden," *Hymns for the Family of God* (Nashville, TN: Paragon Associates, 1976), # 588.

Chapter 10

1 A.W. Tozer, *Keys to the Deeper Life* (Grand Rapids, MI: Zondervan, 1984), p. 29. Used by permission.

2 Talmud, B. Berachoth 3b.

Chapter 11

1 C.S. Lewis, *The Pilgrim's Regress* (New York: Bantam Books, 1981).

Chapter 13

1 John Howe, from the Latin, as quoted by F.B. Meyer, *Some Secrets of Christian Living* (Wilmore, KY: Francis Asbury Press, 1985), p. 38.

Chapter 22

1 John Keble, "Sun of My Soul, Thou Savior Dear," *Hymns of the Christian Life* (Camp Hill, PA: Christian Publications, 1978), # 569.

Chapter 30

1 Dietrich Bonhoeffer, *Life Together* (New York: Harper & Row, 1954), p. 77.

Chapter 31

1 John Bowring, "In the Cross of Christ I Glory," *Hymns of the Christian Life* (Camp Hill, PA: Christian Publications, 1978), # 83.

2 Bernard de Clairvaux, as quoted by F.B. Meyer, *Some Secrets of Christian Living* (Wilmore, KY: Francis Asbury Press, 1985), p. 45.

Chapter 33

1 From "The Great Stone Face," *The Complete Novels and Selected Tales of Nathaniel Hawthorne (1804-1864)*, vol. 2, ed. Norman Holmes Pearson (New York: Random House, 1993).

Chapter 34

1 Mary Lathbury, "Break Thou the Bread of Life," *Hymns of the Christian Life* (Camp Hill, PA: Christian Publications, 1978), # 411.

2 D.A. McGregor, "Jesus, Wondrous Savior," *Hymns of Worship and Remembrance* (Ft. Dodge, IA: Gospel Perpetuating Fund, 1950), # 80.

Chapter 36

1 Helen Lemmel, "Turn Your Eyes upon Jesus," *Hymns of the Christian Life* (Camp Hill, PA: Christian Publications, 1978), # 332.

Chapter 43

1 R.C.H. Lenski, *The Interpretation of St. Paul's Epistle to the Romans* (Minneapolis, MN: Augsburg, 1961), p. 747.

2 Wayne Grudem, *Systematic Theology* (Grand Rapids, MI: Zondervan, 1994), pp. 189-190.

Chapter 44

1 Title and author unknown, as quoted in a sermon by J.R.W. Stott.

2 Handley C.G. Moule, Bishop of Durham, *Keswick Hymn-book* (Toronto: Marshall, Morgan and Scott: n.d.), # 47.

Chapter 52

1 Stefan Lorant, *The Life of Abraham Lincoln* (New York: McGraw-Hill Book Co., 1954; republished 1955 as a Signet Key Book), p. 220. From Abraham Lincoln's second inaugural address.

Chapter 55

1 Stefan Lorant, *The Life of Abraham Lincoln* (New York: McGraw-Hill Book Co., 1954; republished 1955 as a Signet Key Book), p. 220. From Abraham Lincoln's second inaugural address.

Chapter 56

1 J.R.W. Stott, "Lectures on Ephesians" at Regent College Summer School (Vancouver, BC), 1979.

Chapter 59

1 Derek Kidner, *The Proverbs,* The Tyndale Old Testament Commentaries (Downers Grove, IL: InterVarsity, 1964), p. 61.

Chapter 61

1 See D. Martyn Lloyd-Jones, *Studies in the Sermon on the Mount,* vol. II (Grand Rapids, MI: Eerdmans, 1959), 77-78.

Epilogue

1 A.W. Tozer, *The Pursuit of God* (Camp Hill, PA: Christian Publications, 1982, 1993), p. 91.

Rabbit Trail #1

1 Thomas Binney, *Christian Praise* (London: Tyndale Press, 1957, repr. 1968), # 340.

Rabbit Trail #3

1 A.W. Tozer, *The Pursuit of God* (Camp Hill, PA: Christian Publications, 1982, 1993), pp. 12-13.

Keith A. Price is the recipient of several civic honors, including the Chairman of the 1976 Montreal Olympics Christian Activities and Canada's Centennial Medal. A regular columnist in *Faith Today*, Canada's leading interdenominational magazine, Dr. Price presently is minister-at-large with the Evangelical Fellowship of Canada, preaching and teaching to more than forty denominations worldwide. Keith and his wife, Rosemary, reside in Victoria, B.C., Canada.